SELECTED LETTERS

Federico García Lorca

SELECTED LETTERS

Edited
and translated by
David Gershator

A NEW DIRECTIONS BOOK

a newspaper, magazine,
eproduced in any
g photocopying and
tem, without per-

PQ6613.A763 Z48 1983
Garcia Lorca, Federico,
1898-1936.
Selected letters

me of these letters

Lorca family.

Manufactured in the United States of America
First published clothbound and as New Directions Paperbook 557 in 1983.
Published simultaneously in Canada by George J. McLeod, Ltd., Toronto

Library of Congress Cataloging in Publication Data
García Lorca, Federico, 1898–1936.
    Selected letters.
    (A New Directions Book)
    Includes bibliographical references.
    1. García Lorca, Federico, 1898–1936—Correspondence.
    2. Authors, Spanish—20th century—Correspondence.
    I. Gershator, David.   II. Title.
PQ6613.A763Z48   1983   868′.6209 [B]   83-4006
ISBN 0-8112-0872-9
ISBN 0-8112-0873-7 (pbk.)

New Directions Books are published for James Laughlin
by New Directions Publishing Corporation
80 Eighth Avenue, New York 10011

Introduction

Federico García Lorca's letters enable us to meet the most popular Spanish poet and playwright of the twentieth century and become part of his world. We have in the letters an unintentional self-portrait, at times a much more intimate portrait than any biographer could achieve. We see Lorca involved in a process of self-creation and artistic exploration as he embarks on a literary life, and, since he often includes poems and selections of works-in-progress in his letters, we follow the trajectory of his projects from age twenty to a month before his execution at thirty-nine.

The images Lorca projects of himself to friends and acquaintances offer multiple insights into his character and personality. We are privy to the secrets, the awkward moments and happy occasions, the depressions and triumphs, the psychological stresses and cryptic confessions that inevitably come to light in private correspondence. For the most part, the letters are lively and spontaneous. While Lorca tends to a colloquial idiom and style, we also encounter inspired runs of prose and, not surprisingly, streaks of lyricism that reveal the artist in the man. In his early letters, when he does indulge in literary preening and posturing, he appears slightly foolish, especially when he tries to impress the ladies or the other unseasoned young men in his student circle. But such awkwardness is the prerogative of youth.

One question naturally comes to mind: would Lorca approve of the publication of his letters? I believe he would find it flattering. Like most writers, he would have wanted to delete passages, edit, and elucidate, but, all in all, it is likely that his approval would be wholehearted. Why not? He delighted in himself and his friends. He was outgoing and gregarious. He thrived on attention, and center stage in company was his favorite location.

Lorca had a personality that demanded and held attention through the force of its Andalusian color and charm. He easily dominated his circle with his musical talent and poetic high jinks. A member of his generation, the poet Jorge Guillén, used to say to his companions on seeing Lorca approaching: "Here comes Federico, now we can go on a spree of poetry."

Pablo Neruda, the great Chilean poet, remembers him this way:

> To recall him, to capture his photograph at such a distance, is impossible. He was a physical lightning, an energy in constant rapidity, a happiness, a brilliance, a tenderness entirely super-human. His person was magical and dark and brought cheer.[1]

And the Chilean diplomat, Carlos Morla Lynch, who was Lorca's close friend in Spain during the years 1928 to 1936, portrays him similarly:

> Federico: exuberant, vibrant, undisciplined, effervescent; a volcano in constant eruption. Uncontainable force of violent and unexpected outbursts. Altogether the enchantment of a big, playful and mischievous child.[2]

Lorca was endowed with great gifts of person and rejoiced in them, conscious of his winning social talents. However, one popular study of the poet, published in Barcelona, remarks that, from his letters

> . . . one deduces a store of exasperating egotism. There isn't one letter to male friends in which he doesn't seek a favor or petition—generous, egotistical petition—for an article for one of his publications.
> . . . there is always the need, although at times disguised, to call attention to himself, the itch to explain what his projects and ambitions are and to constantly provoke an interest in the things in which he is directly involved.[3]

These are hasty judgments based on the limited number of letters found in the edition collected by Sebastián Gasch. Most of the letters are the normal interchange to be expected between literary friends. From the wider perspective of the letters we now

[1] Pablo Neruda, *Hora de España*, No. 3, p. 65.
[2] Carlos Morla Lynch, *En España con Federico García Lorca*, Madrid, 1957, p. 60.
[3] Sebastián Gasch, *Federico García Lorca: Cartas a sus amigos*, Barcelona, 1950, p. 11.

possess, Lorca's outstanding personality characteristics emerge: he was supportive, sympathetic, generous, demanding, devout, whimsical, insecure, sensitive, and, since he was an Andalusian, punctilious regarding the formalities.

In addition to his natural gifts, Lorca enjoyed financial ease. He did feel family pressure to choose a profession, but as the elder son of a wealthy Granadan landowner, he was given the opportunity to explore his talents and inclinations. He toyed with the idea of a professorial career, but his chosen metier was poetry and theater, and what pride of accomplishment is revealed when the theater finally paid off financially, and he could talk of building his own house on the Mediterranean and jauntily proclaim in a letter to Guillén: "Now it's my turn to earn money."

Lorca (b. 1898) was not an isolated figure. He was a leading member of a generation of poets, a modern Pléiade born around the turn of the century, which became known among Spanish literary historians as the "Generation of '27." Following the European quest for chronological order, the name was applied after the Góngora tricentenary celebration in which all the poets participated. In this mutually nurturing coterie we find Lorca's friends, rivals, and the recipients of his letters: Guillén, Rafael Alberti, Vicente Aleixandre, Luis Cernuda, José Bergamín, Gerardo Diego, Pedro Salinas, and Manolo Altolaguirre, among others.

Lorca's correspondence often appears in concentrated bursts of enthusiasm: with Barcelona critic Sebastián Gasch in 1927–28; with critic and journalist Guillermo de Torre in 1927; with Colombian poet Jorge Zalamea in 1928; and with the Chilean diplomat in Madrid, Carlos Morla Lynch, in 1931. On the other hand, Lorca kept up sustained exchanges over an enduring span of years with fellow poet Jorge Guillén and childhood friend Melchor Fernández Almagro. It is interesting to watch the evolving relationship with Jorge Guillén, the younger Lorca first seeking out the older academic poet with much deference and later relating to him as family friend and peer. But the letters to Melchor, though he was five years Lorca's senior, are always those of social equals.

We know that additional correspondence is still extant— Lorca's letters to his family, for example, of which two are given in this collection. Other letters, like those to Pablo Neruda and

Vicente Aleixandre, were destroyed or lost during the Spanish Civil War.[4] An extensive correspondence existed between Rafael Alberti and Lorca, but only one minor example survives. There are additional letters, unavailable at present, to Gerardo Diego, Antonio Luna, Alfonso García Valdecasas, and many others. Following past patterns, letters will probably surface from time to time.[5]

Some of the earliest letters in this collection date back to Lorca's Residencia de Estudiantes days in Madrid. The Residencia was a university patterned along English lines. The admission requirements limited its facilities mostly to the elite so that it was a type of new Oxford in Spain. Lorca came to this innovative institution when he was twenty-one. The Residencia was a stimulating hothouse for intellectual growth, hosting such distinguished academicians as Ramón Menéndez Pidal and Ortega y Gasset, and guest speakers such as the poets Max Jacob, Paul Valéry, Louis Aragon, and the scientist Marie Curie. In this avant-garde atmosphere Lorca, obviously not very interested in formal study, was able to develop his social and literary talents among an appreciative audience. At the Residencia he met Guillermo de Torre, who was to edit his complete works, the poet José Bergamín, and Salvador Dalí.

Dalí left a descriptive testimonial of his encounter with Lorca:

> . . . The personality of García Lorca produced an immense impression on me. The poetic phenomenon in its entirety and "in the raw" presented itself before me suddenly in flesh and bone, confused, blood-red, viscous and sublime, quivering with a thousand fires of darkness and of subterranean biology like all matter endowed with originality of its own form.[6]

In short, Dalí was overwhelmed. He later confessed to jealousy and described how he avoided the group in which Lorca reigned. Nevertheless, they were to become fast friends until their break in 1928. Lorca stayed in Cadaqués as Dalí's house guest several

---

[4] Lorca's substantial correspondence with Salvador Dalí has apparently been lost; Dalí's letters to Lorca appear in Antonina Rodrigo's *Lorca-Dalí,* Barcelona, 1981.

[5] The most complete Spanish edition of the letters to date is: F. García Lorca, *Epistolario,* ed. Christopher Maurer, Madrid, 1983.

[6] Salvador Dalí, *The Secret Life of Salvador Dali,* New York, 1942, p. 176.

times, which occasioned the delightful letters to Dalí's younger sister, Ana María. Replete with memories, sentiments, childlike plays on words, lyric descriptions, even a private language, they are unique in this collection.

García Lorca was always deeply conscious of his Granadan heritage. Madrid and Barcelona were important cities in his life, but his home was Granada and he always came back . . . loving, resenting, intoxicated by it, and confined by its provinciality, as many letters reveal.

It was in Granada that his friendship with Manuel de Falla flourished. The number of letters to Falla hardly reflects the extent of their close relationship. Their communication was usually person to person; Lorca had only to visit the composer up on the hill. Falla had great regard for Lorca's talent and musicianship, and it is one of the tricks of fate that their attempts at collaboration were never fully realized.

Lorca continued studying piano and guitar while reading law at the University of Granada. He took the law degree just for the sake of having a title, an accepted procedure among members of his social class. At this time he also collected, arranged, and performed folk songs from all parts of Spain, becoming an expert in the field. A number of these songs gained widespread popularity, and in the early thirties he recorded songs with the famous "La Argentinita."

Lorca was also a talented artist. He filled his letters with fanciful flourishes and impish designs and often bestowed his drawings, reflecting Cubist and Surreal influences, on friends as gifts. In a letter to Sebastián Gasch he writes:

> Now I'm starting to write and illustrate poems like this one that I'm sending dedicated to you. When a subject is too lengthy or contains a poetically stale emotion, I resolve it with drawing pencils. This makes me happy and is extraordinarily amusing.

In 1927 Lorca held a semi-private exhibition of his drawings—done in pen and ink and colored pencil—at the Dalmau Galleries of Barcelona, an avant-garde establishment which also exhibited the first works of Salvador Dalí. As letters to Gasch confirm, Lorca seriously considered publishing a book of these drawings. The project was not carried out, although quite a few of the drawings appeared in the literary magazines of the time.

In the years 1927 and 1928 Lorca initiated many projects and memorials in which he enthusiastically involved his friends and colleagues. Early in 1928 he joined wholeheartedly in the adventure of publishing the magazine *gallo* (*Rooster*) with a group of young men in Granada who looked up to him as their leader. Much of his surviving correspondence dates from this period, and the letters frequently include requests for articles, poems, and drawings.

The first issue of the magazine contained work by Lorca, Guillén, Dalí, Fernández Almagro, Bergamín, and others. A bit too audacious for the established values, tastes, and provincial mores of Granada, the editors hit the sensitive nerves of the town; *gallo* created a tempest. The second issue appeared two months later in April. Besides the "Anti-Artistic Manifesto" translated from Catalan and signed by Dalí, Sebastián Gasch, and Luis Montanyá, it contained an homage to Picasso by Gasch, a selection of poetry, a study on Arabic themes by José Navarro Pardo, a fragment of a novel-in-progress by the poet's bother Francisco,[7] and two short dialogues by Lorca. In the two months between issues, Granada had regained her usual serenity and indifference. The magazine which had started off so auspiciously was, in the main, ignored. Response to the second issue didn't augur well for the continuation of the magazine, and the projected third issue, which Lorca discussed in letters to Gasch, never materialized.

At this time Lorca was also concerned with the publication of his *Romancero gitano*. With the success of the *Romancero*, the myth of Lorca the Gypsy gained currency, and, in the public mind, his personality became entangled with the intangible gypsy of his own creation. He protests against this vexing identification in his letters to Melchor Fernández Almagro and Jorge Guillén. Concurrently, in his letters to Jorge Zalamea he gives voice to the hurt inflicted by the *banderillas* of fame. Lorca, commiserating with Zalamea's problems, refers several times in these letters to his own spiritual distress.

Some biographers conclude that, in addition to coping with an identity crisis and sudden fame, Lorca's break with Dalí contributed to his depression and turbulent state of mind. In 1928

[7] Federico García Lorca was the eldest of four children: himself, his brother Francisco (Paco), and his sisters Concha and Isabel (Isabelita).

Dalí wrote a long, sharply critical letter to Lorca concerning the *Romancero gitano* which effectively marked the end of their relationship. In it he disparaged Lorca's work, calling it retrogressive, stereotyped, commonplace, and conformist.[8] Those who knew Lorca in this period claim something happened to his *élan vital.* He even stopped reading his poetry in company, a clue to the depth of his mood, and abandoned the gypsy ballad, setting out instead to compose what he termed a new "vein opening poetry."

During this period of spiritual crisis, Lorca made plans to go to New York in the company of Fernando de los Ríos and left Spain in 1929. In New York Lorca haunted Harlem, wandered the streets, played Spanish folk songs at the piano to admiring gatherings of new friends, pretended to learn English, visited Vermont, lectured at Vassar, walked the Brooklyn Bridge at midnight, attended football games, and produced an impressive body of work. His energy level was obviously stimulated by the new environment; he wrote in whole or in part *Poeta en Nueva York, La zapatera prodigiosa, Yerma, Así que pasen cinco años, El Público,* and a filmscript entitled *Viaje a la luna.*

The correspondence dealing with his New York episode begins in his native Granada and ends with a letter written from Columbia University where he spent a good part of 1929–30 as a student resident of John Jay Hall. The letters chronicle feelings of alienation, disaffection, insecurity, and, finally, his rebirth as that "former Federico."

Lorca left New York in the spring of 1930 to visit Cuba, his first contact with Latin America and a high point of his trip to America. Back in Spain Lorca resumed work in the theater and devoted his energies to La Barraca, a traveling theater group which brought classical Spanish theater to the people of the provinces.

An intimate account of this period in Lorca's life appears in *En España con Federico García Lorca* by Carlos Morla Lynch. This selected diary contains letters which reveal a close relationship between Lynch and the poet. Lorca demonstrates in these letters, as in those to Jorge Zalamea, his effusive, tender nature and capacity for empathizing with the pain of others.

[8] Antonina Rodrigo, *García Lorca en Cataluña*, Barcelona, 1975, pp. 262–264.

The isolated letter to the poet Miguel Hernández—like Lorca a victim of the Civil War—was first published in 1958. Until then it was not known that the two poets corresponded. In 1933 Hernández was a virtual unknown, while Lorca already had a great reputation. From this position, Lorca encouraged the younger poet, properly assessing his talent and "vital and luminous strength."

Bodas de sangre, Lorca's first resounding theatrical success at home and in Latin America, premiered in Madrid in 1933. That year he made a triumphal tour of Argentina, staying for six months in Buenos Aires and presenting his repertoire of plays before huge audiences. The South American reception made him a literary star in the Spanish-speaking world.

In his plays and most of his poetry Lorca was never far from his roots, but, as an experimentalist with a strong rebellious streak, he reached farthest into the twentieth century with *Poeta en Nueva York.* In this tumultuous and impassioned work he writes with uncanny and eerie prescience. Oracular winds still whistle through the lines of the "Fable and Round of the Three Friends":

> When the pure forms caved in
> beneath the *cri cri* of the daisies,
> I realized they had murdered me.
> They ransacked the cafés and the cemeteries and the churches,
> they opened the winecasks and the closets,
> they destroyed three skeletons to yank out their gold teeth.
> They could no longer find me.
> They couldn't find me?
> No. They couldn't find me.
> But it was known that the sixth moon fled upstream,
> and that the sea remembered—suddenly!—
> the names of all the drowned.

Lorca was murdered by Granadan Falangists on the morning of August 19, 1936. He became a worldwide symbol of the Republican cause, and during much of the ensuing Francoist suppression his books were banned. Lorca was one of a million sacrifices in the bloodiest episode of Spain's long war with itself, and his grave at Viznar remains unmarked.

—David Gershator

Acknowledgments

At Columbia University in the late fifties, I was fortunate to be one of Francisco García Lorca's students. It was with his gracious permission, guidance, and cooperation that I originally undertook the project of collecting and translating the correspondence of Federico García Lorca, Spain's great poet, dramatist, and Civil War martyr.

In this selection, which includes most of Lorca's substantial correspondence but excludes postcards and brief letters, I have attempted to adhere to the vivacity and colloquial nature of Lorca's style. The translations are based on letters collected in *García Lorca: Cartas, postales, poemas y dibujos* edited by Antonio Gallego Morell (Madrid: Editorial Moneda, 1968), Federico García Lorca, *Obras completas* (Madrid: Aguilar, 1962), *García Lorca en Cataluña* by Antonina Rodrigo (Barcelona: Planeta, 1975), *"Trece de Nieve"* (No. 182, December, 1976), and several other journals published here and abroad. Poems translated or mentioned in the text which are not otherwise noted appear in the latest edition of Federico García Lorca, *Obras completas,* Vol. I (Madrid: Aguilar, 1981). All translations of poems included in this volume are my own. Thanks to Christopher Maurer, editor of F. García Lorca, *Epistolario* (Madrid: Alianza, 1983), it has sometimes been possible to correct the Aguilar text against facsimiles of the original letters. The dates of the letters, whenever different from those given in Aguilar, are those suggested by Maurer and justified in the *Epistolario*.

I am grateful to the following for their help, encouragement, and advice: Manuel Fernández-Montesinos García, Peggy Fox, Prof. Robert Clements, Lehman Weichselbaum, Eliot Weinberger, James Laughlin, Prof. William Rose, Ivan Argüelles, Donald J. Davidson, John Thaxton, Prof. Zenaide Guitiérrez Vega, Mercedes Orbón, the Tinker Library of the Spanish Institute, Prof. Christopher Maurer, the late Francisco García Lorca, and my wife, Phillis Manuela.

In translating, as most translators would admit, the last word is no last word. I can only hope that the words I've chosen add up to an appropriate interpretation of the man, the poet, and his language.

—D. G.

TO MARIA DEL REPOSO URQUIA[1]

[Granada] Night of the 1 [February, 1918]

Esteemed and distant friend:

Perhaps it might seem strange to you that I write you like this, so soon, but, since your diminutive and charming figure never left my imagination, I believe I'm still talking to you. Perhaps it's the ideal correspondence, that of kindred souls. Ah! Don't laugh, don't laugh, Reposo. I dare to write you (and I say I dare, because in Spain these things are daring) to ask you a favor. I'm publishing a book. Would you allow me to dedicate a chapter to you? Answer me, then. . . . I believe you will honor me with your reply. I don't expect anything other than that from a woman like you, an admirer of Chopin and such a good interpreter of his works. There are times, my little friend, when we feel the desire to write to a soul unseen far off in the distance and that that soul hear our call of friendship. In this day and age, we, the romantics, must immerse ourselves in the shadows of a society that exists only within ourselves. Perhaps you are, like me, a romantic who dreams of something very spiritual, that you cannot find. Yes, yes! Don't laugh. Even if it provokes laughter in you (something which I do not believe), that's the way it is, even though you don't want it to be so. We always feel a bitter sorrow we cannot root out. Forgive me if I annoy you . . . , I am too impassioned. . . . I don't wish to annoy you any further. Do you accept? I ask it of you with all my heart. You are one of those women who advance along the road of life leaving a wake of tranquility, of sympathy, of spiritual calm. Something like the perfume of a flower hidden away in the distance. . . . How badly I write, isn't that so? Forgive me. Answer me right away, if you have no objection. I'll be infinitely grateful. You can always rely on me.

Federico García Lorca

(Regards to Paquita)

[1] Maria del Reposa Urquía was a young woman Lorca met and visited in Baeza, probably at the end of 1917. Ian Gibson has published an article about their friendship, "Federico en Baeza," A.B.C., November 6, 1966.

TO ADRIANO DEL VALLE[1]

[May, 1918]

[May today in time and October above my head]

PEACE

Friend:

I was very pleased to receive your letter and you can be sure that it gave me moments of great spiritual satisfaction. I come before you merely as a companion (a companion full of sadness) who has read some of your lovely poems.

I am a poor impassioned and silent fellow who, very nearly like the marvelous Verlaine, bears within a lily impossible to water, and to the foolish eyes of those who look upon me I seem to be a very red rose with the sexual tint of an April peony, which is not my heart's truth. I appear before people (those things that call themselves people as [illegible word] says) like an Oriental drunk on the full moon and I feel like a Chopinesque Gerineldo in an odious and despicable epoch of Kaisers and La Ciervas (down with them!).[2] My image and my verses give the impression of something very passionate . . . and, yet, at the bottom of my soul there's an enormous desire to be very childlike, very poor, very hidden. I see before me many problems, many entrapping eyes, many conflicts in the battle between head and heart and all my sentimental flowering seeks to enter a golden garden and I try hard because I like paper dolls and the playthings of childhood, and at times I lie down on my back on the floor to play games[3] with my kid sister (she's my delight) . . . , but the phantom that lives within us and hates us pushes me down the path. One must move along because we must grow old and die, but I don't want to pay attention to it . . . and, nevertheless, with each day that passes I have another doubt and another sadness. Sadness of the enigma of myself! There is within us, Adriano my friend, a desire not to suffer and an innate goodness, but the external force of temptation and the overwhelming tragedy of physiology insure our destruction. I believe that everything around us is full of the souls that passed on, that they are the ones who provoke our sorrows and that they are the ones who enter the kingdom inhabited by that white and blue virgin

2

called **Melancholy** . . . , or in other words, the kingdom of Poetry (I have no conception of poetry other than the lyric). I entered it a long time ago . . . ; I was ten years old and I fell in love . . . ; and then I immersed myself completely, making my vows to the singular religion of Music and donning the vestments of passion that She lends to those who love her. After I entered the kingdom of Poetry, I ended by anointing myself with love for everything. To sum up, I'm a good boy, who opens his heart to the whole world. . . . Of course I'm a great admirer of France and I hate militarism with all my heart, and feel only an immense desire for Humanity. Why struggle with the flesh while the frightening problem of the spirit exists? I love Venus madly, but even more I love the question, Heart? And most of all, I keep to myself, like that rare and true Peer Gynt with the button moulder . . . ; I want me to be myself.

As for the things I'm doing, I can only tell you that I'm working hard; I write a lot and do a lot of music. I have written three books (two of them poetry) and expect to do more work. As for music, I am now busy taking down the splendid interior polyphony of Granadan folksongs.

As for my first book, I thank you for your praise. Let me tell you that in writing about it you don't have to say anything to me, because once the book hits the streets, it's no longer mine, it's everybody's. . . . In my book (which is very bad) there is only one great emotion that always flows from my sadness and the ache I feel before Nature. . . . I don't know if you can tell how sincere I am, impassioned and humble-hearted. It's enough for me to know that yours is the spirit of a poet. And even if you were unable to see the poor light of my soul that I shed in this letter or even if you should laugh, I would only feel the intimate bitterness of having shown something of my interior reliquary to a soul who closed his eyes and smiled skeptically. Of course I dismiss this. I am a great romantic, and that is my chief pride. In a century of zeppelins and stupid deaths, I sob at my piano dreaming of the Handelian mist and I create verses very much my own, singing the same to Christ as to Buddha, to Mohammed, and to Pan. For a lyre I have my piano and, instead of ink, the sweat of yearning, yellow pollen of my inner lily and my great love. One must kill the "little rich boys" and annul the laughter of those who love Harmony. We must love the moon over the lake of our soul and make our religious meditations over the magnificent abyss of full-blown sunsets . . . , because it colors the music of our eyes. . . . I leave my pen now to board the pious ship of Dreams. Now you know what I'm like in one aspect of my life.

If you wish to answer me, the address is Acera del Casino . . . , though I'm sure my uncle knows it. Give him my warmest greetings. He's very good and very affectionate . . . , but he doesn't know me in depth. For him I've always been a boy who has spoken little, has smiled and nothing more. Forgive me my horrible handwriting. I've been very sincere with you. . . . Read this sad letter, meditate on it, and afterwards I'm sure you'll say ". . . But what a fellow! So young! In short, a poet." And here's my left hand, which is the hand of the heart.

Federico

A favor. . . . Don't ever sing the "Song of the Soldier" (it's the work of a musical barber!); even though they threaten to shoot you. Otherwise you can't be my friend.

---

[1] Adriano del Valle: futurist poet.

[2] Refers to Juan de la Cierva y Peñafiel who, in the elections of 1918, became Minister of War and virtual head of government under García Prieto, causing a national crisis when he intervened militarily in civil affairs.

[3] Lorca uses the phrase "jugar a comadricas." Manuel Fernández-Montesinos García, Lorca's nephew (who graciously answered many queries about textual problems in the letters), explains comadricas as a pejorative diminutive of comadre, meaning a nosy person or gossip, but he does not know exactly what game (if any) Lorca meant.

[Early 1920s]

Due to laziness and nothing more than laziness I haven't answered your letter; I am, then, a scoundrel and a bad friend. I used to get up very sadly every morning and I would go for a walk around this marvelous Granada, come back to eat, start to study and so the afternoon took me by surprise. Who writes to friends in the afternoon . . . ? I think this excuse is sufficient for an artist like you, but rest assured that I remember you with great happiness and associate your specter with three absurd things, which I explain subconsciously: a lower case letter, a few weak curls and some of Koch's bacillus in caricature. Some other day I'll explain this to you. Now I've discovered something awful (don't tell this to anyone). *I haven't been born yet.* The other day I studied my past attentively (I was seated on my grandfather's easy chair) and none of the dead hours belonged to me because it wasn't I who had lived them, neither the hours of love, nor the hours of hate, nor the hours of inspiration. There were a thousand Federico García Lorcas, stretched out forever in the attic of time and in the storehouse of the future. I contemplated another thousand Federico García Lorcas, very tightly pressed, one on top of the other, waiting to be filled with gas in order to fly off without direction. This moment was a terribly fearful moment, my mother Lady Death had given me the key of time and for a second I understood everything. I'm living on borrowed time, what I have within is not mine; let's see if I'm going to be born. My soul definitely has not opened. It's with reason that I sometimes believe I have a tin heart! In short, my dear Regino, I'm sad now and bored by my false interior. I expect your letter immediately and without any grumbling; I don't believe you're vengeful.

An effusive and enormous hug

Federico

Alcalde tells me just now that he received your letter taking leave of your friends; it makes me very sad to see that you don't mention me. Forgive me for not writing you, but I assure you that I keep you close to my heart. Answer me then. Don't be vindictive, I repeat once more. If you could only see what the *sierra* looks like! All red, and from the balconies one glimpses the plain all in shade. Study a lot and don't lie around in bed.—Granada, 16— My brother gives you a manly handshake from here. Goodbye, guitarist. Remember me.

---

[1] Regino Sainz de la Maza: celebrated guitarist.

Asquerosa, 27 [August, 1920]

Dear Antoñito:

Little by little the domestic mole of family love has been under-mining my swaddling-clothed heart, convincing me that I owe it to decency and duty to terminate my shipwrecked career as an Undergraduate. . . . What do you think? My father had already given thought to my going to Madrid in October and my whole family accepted the idea, but accepted with resignation, not as happy as I would wish, because my father is pained to see me with no career other than my *emotion about things.* Yesterday he told me: "Look, Federico, you are free; go wherever you wish, because I am convinced that you have a strong proclivity for the arts; but why don't you give me some satisfaction and finish your studies—in whatever way you'd like. Does that sound difficult? If you'd pass some subjects this September, I'd let you go to Madrid with more happiness than if you'd made me emperor."

So you see, dear friend, how right my father is, and since he's already old and he would like me to adorn myself with a career, my decision is final. I'm going to finish up! Since poor [Martín Domínguez] Berrueta has died (it would have made me feel un-comfortable to have him give me my exams), I will register again, although as a free student,[2] in my "alma mater."

And here is my question: What shall I do? I'm working on two theater pieces now: a poem "The Baby Poplars" and, as always, my lyrical poetry. Must I, Antoñito of my heart and soul, aban-don my children without raising them, tears of my spirit and flesh of my heart, to caress the cold tomes of dead histories and moribund concepts? Or will I be able to bear both weightless burdens? I still have to pass everything from Universal History onward. What subjects will I be able to pass? Do you think it's all right if I take History, Paleography (which ought to be easy) and Numismatics? Where am I sure to pass and with whom? It's not that I don't want to work (since I am already suffering and that's work), but it's a big bother, and to you—my savior!—I turn.

What I'd like to do is to show my father a few passing grades in September to make him happy and I will go off with a clear conscience to publish my books and study the elements of Philosophy with *Pepe Ortega*[3] at a leisurely pace, something he has promised me.

Answer me by return mail with the necessary instructions and what's really happening. And are Hebrew and Arabic really as easy as pie with [José] Navarro [Pardo]? (How in the world can I ever learn Hebrew or Arabic?) (They must pass me immediately!) Since you are an Instructor in the Faculty [of Arts and Science], you should be well informed about subjects, professors and [crossed out] and (oh, grammar!) incompatibilities.

Seriously, I'd be eternally grateful, and I hope you'll treat me as I wish and hope. Be so kind then as to answer immediately.

The country is magnificent—why don't you come out some day?—and I with the whole countryside lodged too deeply in my soul. If you could see those sunsets so full of spectral dew . . . , that afternoon dew, that seems to descend for the dead and for lovers gone astray which amounts to the same thing! If you could see that melancholy of pensive canals and those rotating rosaries of water wheels! I expect the country to polish my lyrical branches this blessed year with the red knives of afternoons.

Until your next letter a close embrace from your student-poet and pianist-gypsy friend,

Federico

Answer me immediately!
Your address:
    Asquerosa.
    (By Pinos Puente.)
    Granada.
Hugs from my brother!

[1] Antonio Gallego Burín: Granadan writer, editor, and critic—two years older than Lorca.
[2] Manuel Montesinos describes a "free student" as one who has the right to take exams but does not have to attend class.
[3] An irreverent reference to José Ortega y Gasset (1883–1955): major philosopher of the twentieth century; author of *Meditaciones del Quijote, La deshumanización del arte,* and *La rebelión de las masas.* Lorca refers to him—as though to a gypsy bullfighter or flamenco singer—as *Pepe Ortega.*

TO ADRIANO DEL VALLE

Today 19 [September, 1920]

My dear friend Adriano:

I'm sure I must have acquired a terrible reputation as a bad and lazy friend in your eyes . . . , but forgive me! I've gone through a crisis of distances and sorrows that not even I was aware of. One can say that I was a shadow drunk with summer and impossible passion. . . . I had in my soul, in that unfathomable well from which St. Theresa built her inner castle, a layer of sonorous spikes of wheat and white clouds.

I've contemplated the blue sky too much and I have felt real wounds of light. . . . Along the roads of the Granadan Plain [the *Vega*] I thought of no one, not even myself. In my meditations with the poplars and the waters, I've arrived at the Franciscan stance of Francis Jammes.[1] . . . I understand that all of this is very lyrical, too lyrical, but lyricism is what will save me before eternity. Besides, we're in an overwhelming lake of vulgarity and I want my fantastic caravel to travel across it toward the temple of the Exquisite with its sails billowing with snow and sun. I'm like a dream made flesh, and though my horizon is lost in formidable twilights of passions, I have like Prometheus a chain I find hard to drag along. . . . Not that I'm chained to the rocks . . . , but, instead of an eagle, an owl tears at my heart. All of this is sincere. Total sincerity! To say anything else would be ridiculous and grotesque. I feel full of poetry, strong poetry, simple, fantastic, religious, bad, deep, wicked, mystical. Everything, everything, I want to be all things. Well do I know that the dawn keeps a hidden key in strange forests, but I'll know how to find it. . . . Have you read Unamuno's[2] latest essays? Read them; you'll enjoy them tremendously. . . .

I've worked a great deal this summer.

I've done a poem in verse about the Plain of Granada, which will probably see the light this coming summer, but before that I have to publish two books of poetry titled *True Elegies* [*Elegias verdaderas*] and *Poem of the Infant Autumn* [*Poema del otoño infantil*]. I don't know whether I'll change the titles later; in this I'm very odd, but that's what I think right now.

The first one will be out in November. Right now I'm involved in my work *St. Francis of Assisi,* which is something completely new and strange. I'll send a manuscript of my verses and prose for you to publish. One request. Few and select contributors. Don't compromise on the things you publish. Literature is literature, and he who tries by any means to be a literary figure shows himself to be a fool of the first order. Life is full of roads and on all of them there are bitter and sweet things to be found.

I'll send you one of the latest things I've done, "The Elegy of the Toads."

As always among friends, I'll subscribe to the magazine . . . I would tell you many things, but I feel no inclination to speak. In my soul is a forest full of nests which come to life with the breeze of my great passion.

Forgive me Adriano. May the divine Apollo save you.

Federico

I'll send you my book. Answer me.

---

[1] Francis Jammes (1868–1938): French poet and novelist known for his spiritual involvement with nature.

[2] Miguel de Unamuno (1864–1936): novelist, philosopher, essayist.

TO EMILIA LLANOS MEDINA

[Madrid, November 25, 1920][1]

[Miss Emilia Llanos
Granada. Plaza Nueva 1.]

My friend Emilia:

I ask your pardon for the way I've behaved with you, who are so enchanting and exquisite. . . . But I know that Emilia always forgives because she's a good friend of mine. Right? I work a lot and live far less than I could, but the moon is beautiful and there are blue stars. . . . I live the chaste song of my heart.

I'll be writing you at leisure and at length. Answer me, for God's sake, I ask you on my knees, at the Residencia de Estudiantes [Students' Residence], Pinar, 15, my present address.

Adiós, enchanting Emilia. You have not been forgotten by your loyal

Federico

[1] Written in pencil at the end of a letter from the painter Ismael González de la Serna to Emilia Llanos Medina, Lorca's Granadan friend and companion, twelve years his senior.

TO EMILIA LLANOS MEDINA

[Madrid, November 28, 1920]

[Miss Emilia Llanos
Plaza Nueva. Granada.]

Dear Emilia:

It's been a long time since I've heard anything about you and yesterday I recalled you affectionately as I do when it comes to people as refined and as spiritual as you are.

I see you in the midst of that marvelous Granadan landscape as the only Granadan woman capable of feeling it, and it makes me extraordinarily happy to have a friend who looks at the burnished poplars and the faint distances as I would look at them.

How beautiful and sad must be the way of the Darro [River] and what clouds must hang over Valparaíso! Right? I remember Granada as one must remember bygone sweethearts and as one recalls a sunlit day of childhood. Have all the leaves fallen? . . . Here, in Madrid, all the trees are skeletal and cold; on only a few does a little leaf remain, and it moves in the sad wind like a golden butterfly.

It's beginning to rain now and everything is covered by a marvelous mist.

I . . . , to be frank, I am a trifle sad, a trifle melancholy; in my soul I feel the bitterness of being bereft of love. I know that these melancholy thoughts will pass . . . , but the telltale sign remains forever!

Yesterday I went down the Carrera de San Jerónimo and I saw a woman who looked like you: the same height, the same elegance. And the most amusing thing was that she stopped at an antique store. . . . And what antiques! . . . Chinese jars, old pottery, Japanese vases, Indian necklaces. . . . You would have cried out loud and Genoveva [Genoveva Rodríguez de Arrufat], the store owner, would have come out in fright.

Would you be so kind as to send me your signed picture so I can look at it often? Will you do it? I'll repay you with a poem. . . . Is it a deal?

Nothing more to tell you for today. I am punctilious and await your answer in order to write you at greater length.

Adiós, Emilia. Your friend does not forget you

Federico

Regards to Federiquito.[1]

---

[1] Federico Tegeiro Llanos: Emilia Llanos' nephew.

TO MELCHOR FERNANDEZ ALMAGRO

[Asquerosa, Summer of 1921?]

Dear Melchorito:

From this retreat in the center of the [Granadan] plain, I remember you with a deep affection you should never doubt.

When I arrived you can't imagine the great happiness I felt on seeing the tremulous plain in a delirium of blue mist . . . and I felt (you can believe it) true horror recalling terrible things like *Arenal Street, Pardiñas.*

I believe I belong among these melodic poplars and lyrical rivers, with their continuous still waters, because my heart is truly at ease and I laugh at my passions which in the tower of the city attack me like a herd of panthers.

Asquerosa is one of the prettiest towns of the plain on account of its whiteness and the serenity of its inhabitants.

I'm very happy surrounded by my family, who love me so much, and I am working a lot with good results. I'm beginning to like my poems!

As yet nothing has been said about my book and I believe it's because they haven't finished sending them out, because only yesterday (!) the first copies arrived in Granada.[1] I would be grateful from the bottom of my heart if you would do an article in Granada, since I'm not thinking of giving it to just anybody, and nobody, except you, can speak of my verses with deep feeling. I hope you'll do it.

If you see [José] Mora [Guarnido] tell him I'm in love with Marichu Zamora and I keep the innocent hieroglyphs of her tinkling laughter close to my heart. I hope you'll write me immediately, since I want to *correspond* with you this summer in order to organize the Magazine, for which I have many hopes.

In my house they remember Mora with a great deal of affection; tell that to him, and as soon as he answers me I'll write him.

You can't imagine how much my uncle Enrique[2] likes you and how much he wants to see you. There are few such admirers, Melchorito!

Regards from my father and sisters and brother, and a big hug for you from this poet who loves you

Federico

Address: Asquerosa (Pinos Puente).
Adiós and long live Aht![3]
I am starting to give birth to "The Death of the Dauro."

[1] *Libro de poemas* (*Book of Poems*), Madrid, 1921.
[2] Enrique García Rodríguez, his father's brother.
[3] Lorca is imitating the way Angel Barrios pronounced the word "art" (*alte* instead of *arte*).

TO MELCHOR FERNANDEZ ALMAGRO

[Granada, Summer, 1921]

My dear Melchorito:

I said I would write you and I haven't (very bad, right?), but this doesn't mean that my affection for you is any less or that I have forgotten you. Everybody knows how much I love and admire you, and you ought to know it, too.

This letter has no other purpose than to say: what about the Magazine? I'm enthusiastic about the idea, and no matter how much cold water they'll throw on us (which they will), we will not relent.

I've gotten *sixty* subscriptions among the *refined* people of Granada, always making sure that they're young; so almost all the subscribers belong to the aristocracy of the University. We can, therefore, dear Melchorito, do *advance* work among this young crowd. As for myself, I'm crazy with happiness; I hope you will be, too, and that your enthusiasm for this work won't let up. [Adolfo] Salazar is enthusiastic; also Roberto Gerhard, Manolo [Angeles] Ortiz and all those who care *deeply* about a magazine that would make us live more intensely, a magazine that would unite us and would advance gallantly in this sad period of mediocre and *mean-spirited* people.

I'll contribute with what I can; besides, I've gotten many, the majority of these Granadans, to pay a *peseta* and even two *pesetas* per issue as patrons, a sufficiently modest sum it seems to me.

Start to think up interesting things and start gathering subscriptions.

The title? We'll figure one out!

Answer me immediately. This time I intend to answer you, so you know how much I'm interested in it. I don't want to do anything else except talk about the Magazine, *with a capital letter "M."*

Adiós, Melchor. As always, your loving and re-loving

Federico

Your sister's fine, right?

TO ADOLFO SALAZAR

[Asquerosa] Tuesday, 2 [August, 1921]

Dear Adolfo:

I've just gotten your letter and I'm answering immediately—and gratefully, as you can well imagine.

Your article seems the epitome of high praise and good taste.[1] Many thanks, Adolfo! Many thanks! I don't deserve so much, and therefore I'm doubly grateful. The only way to repay you is to tell you that as you already know my affection is sincere, and my heart will always be loyally yours.

I'm completely in agreement with you about the things *in my book that you toss back at me*. There are many more! But I saw that beforehand. . . . What's bad stands out . . . , but, dear Adolfo, when the poems were at the printers they seemed to me (or they seem to me) all equally bad. Manolo [Angeles Ortiz] can tell you of the bad times I've had . . . , but there was no choice! If you only knew! I don't find myself in my book, I'm lost in the terrible fields of the essay, leading my heart, full of tenderness and simplicity, along the declamatory path, by the path of humor, by the *indecisive path,* until at last I think I've found an ineffable little road full of daisies and multicolored lizards.

You can imagine how oppressive I find those terrible verses that you cite if I tell you that there isn't a single copy of the book in my house! I feel as if I hadn't published it. And, were it not for my parents (who say I'm a failure because no one talks about me), I wouldn't have said anything to you about sending me reviews, etc. etc. But my family which is displeased with me because I haven't passed my subjects, is clearly pleased that the book is talked about. I'm thinking of writing to Peinado Chica, *my administrator,* to send books to the newspapers and we'll finish up once and for all, since I have high hopes for the work I'm doing now, which seems to me the best and most exquisite I've produced, so that by autumn it will see the light. If you see [Enrique Díez-] Canedo, let him know, and if he doesn't want to do it [a review], let him go to the devil, since I'm not asking anything that isn't fair and normal.

If you could only see how I remember you! There are friendships that slip through the fingers like clear water, others are like a rose that one absent-mindedly sticks in his lapel, but true friendships are like the [leather] *suction cups* of Andalusian children, they are limpets placed silently over the heart.

Especially when I hear singing I remember you in a tidal rush. Everywhere they sing and what songs! Everyday I'm convinced more and more of how marvelous this country is. If you were here with me you'd be spinning like a top to see the four points of the compass at the same time.

A few days ago a purple-green moon came out over the bluish mist of the Sierra Nevada and in front of my door a woman sang a *berceuse* that was like a golden streamer entangling the whole countryside. Especially at twilight one lives in the fullest fantasy, a half erased dream. . . . There are times when everything evaporates and we're left in a desert of pearl gray, of rose and dead silver. I can't describe to you the vastness of this plain and this little white village in the midst of dark poplar groves.

At night our very flesh hurts from so many bright stars and we get drunk on wind and water. I doubt that in India there are nights so laden with aroma and so delirious. And, naturally, I remember you as I remember all those *close to me* and I'm hoping that you will come through here.

Besides, don't you know? I'm learning to play the guitar. It seems to me that the *flamenco* style is one of the most gigantic creations of the Spanish people. I can already accompany *fandangos, peteneras* and the song style of the gypsies: *tarantas, bulerías* and *romeras*. Every afternoon el Lombardo (a marvelous gypsy) and Frasquito er de La Fuente (another splendid gypsy) come to teach me. Both sing and play in an inspired fashion reaching the deepest layers of popular expression. You can see I'm having a good time.

I'm working a lot now and I believe you'll like what I'm doing, since it seems better to me than the *Suites* which you already know. Do you want me to send you something? I'm titling these things "songs with reflection," because that alone is what I want: to render in words the sublime sensations of a reflection, removing from the tremor whatever it has of Baroque undulations. I'm also creating yellowish ballads, and a very small devotional in honor of our immortal father Sirius; . . . in short, I'm busy enough.

I'm pounding away at the Billy Club Puppets. I ask everybody and they're giving me a slew of enchanting details. They've disappeared by now from these towns, but the things the old people remember are extremely picturesque and would make you fall down laughing. Just imagine one of the scenes where a shoemaker called *Currito er der Puerto* wants to take the measure of a pair of boots for Miss Rosita, and she doesn't want to for fear of Cristóbal, but Currito is very persistent and convinces her by singing this couplet in her ear:

> *Rosita, to see*
> *the tip of your foot,*
> *if I catch you,*
> *you'll see what I'll do,*

with a melody of stupendous vulgarity: but Cristóbal comes along and clubs him to death.[2]

Everytime this jealous Hercules ties up his victim he says: "One, two, and three, into the ravine with him!" and one hears a formidable drumbeat from the depths of the little theater.

Isn't it amusing? Tell me what you're planning to do, and I will surprise you right away.

As for your *tantrums* I listen to them with great pleasure, since in some things you're very right, but in your letter there are two or three things that I don't completely understand and I'd like you to explain what you mean by "the sharpest darts of some of your friends." Explain it to me!

Everything else you tell me is true, a bitter truth. I see life is now casting its chains upon me. Life has its reason, too much reason, but . . . my wings, what a pity! My dried-up childhood, what a pity!

Here in the village I'm very much loved by the laborers, especially by the boys, with whom I walk and talk and everything.

I'll be in Granada when you return and we will go around everywhere. As for Roberto [Gerhard] I would be overjoyed if he were to visit.

I haven't gotten *Indice* and I'm saddened and anguished by the problems of Gabriel [García Maroto], whom I love as you can't imagine, since he deserves it, he is so good and so impassioned. I haven't behaved towards him as well as he deserves, but I assure you that the fault wasn't mine.

Write me as soon as possible, since by now you know how happy your letters make me, and you know how wholeheartedly I love you:

Federico

How is Juan José? Give him a hug for me. *Adiós.*

---

[1]*"Un poeta nuevo. Federico G. Lorca"* which appeared in *El Sol,* July 30, 1921. Salazar appreciatively reviewed *Libro de poemas* and notes the main trends in Lorca's poetry at this early stage. He also criticizes the "inevitable reminiscences," the "forced attempts," and the "high sounding and artificial expressions" in the poet's first book of poetry. Salazar was a noted essayist, musicologist, and composer.

[2]Cristóbal is the Iberian Punch. This episode appears later in the *Tragicomedia de don Cristóbal y la Señá Rosita.*

TO MELCHOR FERNANDEZ ALMAGRO

[Asquerosa, August, 1921]

Dear Melchorito:

Now I really do call you perfidious! You haven't answered. . . . Are you ill?

You don't know how much I'd like it if you'd write me long and leisurely letters talking about everything. . . . Why not about our (*our!*) magazine? I'm leaving for Madrid on the 25th or 26th of September and we've got to form a group of good and determined friends who, out of love and friendship (which is the case at the Little Corner),[1] will *do something serious.* This year I'm very restless; I can't stand being here another minute and I've got to fly, fly, far away . . . and, most of all, to act in a manner worthy of that dandyish and absurd Madrid. The Magazine (with a capital letter M) must be done. We'll get money wherever we can, but we've got to do it! Are we going to carry out what we've been *tossing back and forth*? And, above all, we've got to give a *drubbing to Mariana.* You know who Mariana is! I believe that *we can count on* (besides the governor) all of the *best* and some of the *worst* who are sufficiently sympathetic.

I'm starting to work and am writing some prose pieces, badly written, probably, but full of hope. In verse I'm writing some "little tales of the wind." . . . We'll see! . . . But how admirable and full of perspectives the wind is!

Here go two little presents (two puff pastries of wind!):

ROSE

Compass rose!
(Metamorphosis
of the black point.)
Compass rose!
(Point in blossom.
Open point.)

And this one:

SCHOOL

TEACHER
What maiden marries
the wind?

CHILD
The maid of all
desires.

TEACHER
What does the wind
give her?

CHILD
Golden whirlwinds
and the maps above.

TEACHER
Does she offer anything?

CHILD
Her open heart.

TEACHER
Say her name.

CHILD
Her name is a secret.
(The school
window
has a curtain
of stars).

What do you think? . . . There are many other things, and if you're not perfidious and slick as a wave and answer me by return mail, I will send you lots of verses that are special by virtue of their being unpublished for anybody but you.

I'm in the country enjoying Nature and listening to the immortal crickets sharpening their little golden blades.

Listen: What about [José de] Ciria [y Escalante] the *Apollonian*? If he's in Madrid tell him to write me.

Greetings from me to anybody you run into who asks about me.

To the great Ramón [Gómez de la Serna], best regards.

A hug for you from

Federico

I am in Arquerosa (we've changed the name) by way of Pinos Puente.[2]

---

[1] The Little Corner, *"El rinconcillo,"* refers to the group of young artists and intellectuals that met at the Alameda Café in Granada.

[2] "Asquerosa" means vomitacious, so Lorca and his circle tried to change the name to Arquerosa. In 1941, the name of the town was officially changed to Valderrubio.

TO MELCHOR FERNANDEZ ALMAGRO

Dear Melchorito:

Long live *Aht*!

I received your letter in bed, and I'm getting up today to answer you in this *shord* but affectionate letter.

I've suffered some terrible neuralgia and fevers; besides my teeth hurt . . . In short, *dodalled*. As soon as I *ged bedder* I'll be *leavink*.[1]

I think what you've done with the Magazine is wonderful, but I wish you'd answer me immediately and tell me about my dear friend Gabriel's[2] projects and everything else. I'm impatient.

Granada pales at times and in the streets that face the fields there's an infinite desolation and the murmur of an abandoned port.

Autumn changes the plain into a submerged bay. In the tower of the Alhambra, haven't you felt the urge to sail off? Haven't you seen the ideal ships sleepily bobbing at the foot of the towers? Today I realize, in the midst of this pearly gray sunset, that I live in a marvelous Atlantis.

I'd like to leave but I don't, however, want to leave until everything turns golden.

The valleys of the Darro and the Genil in this autumn season are the only paths in this world that would take us to the *land of Nowhere,* which must lie among those murmuring mists.

I'm neither sad nor happy; I'm inside autumn; I am . . .

> . . . Oh, heart, heart!
> Cupid's Saint Sebastián! . . .

In short, Melchorito, write me immediately, don't delay, and tell me everything. Give [Gabriel García] Maroto a big silent hug from me and another for you from

Federico

Is this *Duesday* or *Dursday?*

Regards from my family and friends who remember you; a hug from my brother Paquito.

[1] Lorca is again making gentle fun of Angel Barrios's pronunciation (*colta* for *corta, er cormo* for *el colmo, le ponga* for *reponga,* and *ilme* for *irme*), while at the same time imitating how he now sounds with a bad cold.
[2] The painter and printer Gabriel García Maroto, who published Lorca's *Libro de poemas.*

TO ADOLFO SALAZAR

[Granada, January 1, 1922]

NEW YEAR'S

Dear Adolfo:

Why have I taken so long to write you? . . . Well, because I was ill-humored, ill-humored because I wasn't in Madrid with you, and ill-humored . . . weary from so much beauty: All the most marvelous themes I've ever envisioned in my life have filled my dancing heart these last months . . . , and it was not possible to *create them* all. Isn't it true that's reason enough to be in a bad mood? But I'm always thinking of you. [Manuel de] Falla can vouch for it. I've been across the green waters of neuralgia two times, but fortunately I'm fine now, and I expect that after Epiphany you'll see me in Madrid. (Over the desk on which I write one sees the Sierra Nevada.)

My silence has been necessary . . . , I've imposed it on myself. Why scratch the little wounds I bear beneath my tunic? Right?

By now *you probably know* of the *Cante Jondo* competition. It's an idea of ours that seems admirable to me because of the enormous importance it has within the artistic and popular field. I am enthusiastic! Have you signed the document? I didn't want to sign it until the last minute, because my signature has no importance . . . , but I had to practically get down on my knees in front of Manuelito [Manuel de Falla] in order to get his, and I finally got it. That's what I should have done, right? You don't know how happy it makes me that that man *Juan* [Jean Aubry] is translating a few of my poems, and especially when I know that you are the *engineer*.[1]

If you could only see how much I've worked! . . . I've just *gone over* the *Suites* for the last time, and now I'm putting the little golden roof tiles on the *Poem of the Cante Jondo,* which I'll publish to coincide with this competition. It's distinct from the *Suites* and full of Andalusian implications. Its rhythm is *stylized popular* and I make the old *singers* shine in them and all the fauna and fantastic flora that fills those sublime songs: Silverio, Juan Breva, Loco Mateo, la Parrala, el Fillo . . . and

Death! It's an altarpiece . . . , it is . . . a *jigsaw puzzle,* do you understand? The poem starts out with an immobile sunset and through it parade the *siguiriya,* the *solea,* the *saeta* and the *petenera.*[2] The poem is full of gypsies, oil lamps, anvils; it even has allusion to Zoroaster. It's the first of *another orientation of mine* and I don't know yet what to tell you about it . . . , but it does have novelty! The only one who knows about it is Falla and he's enthusiastic. . . . And you'll understand that very well knowing *Manué* [Manuel de Falla] and knowing how crazy he is about these things. The Spanish poets have never *touched* this theme, and just for the daring I deserve a smile, which you'll send me immediately.

Yesterday I wired a 100 *pesetas* to *Indice,* 50 as my quota and 50 that I'm giving from my *New Year's gifts.* I'm very happy with the Magazine. Tomorrow I'll be sending you several originals for the *finger,*[3] and you, or Juan Ramón [Jiménez], will choose. It's all the same to me. There are more than thirty subscriptions, but I've got to go house to house to collect the money. Give my regards to Juan Ramón and all our friends. Tell [José de] Ciria [y Escalante] that when he goes to Madrid in January he shouldn't even greet me, since I don't think I want to talk to him any more. Undoubtedly people aren't *like oneself; one* is foolish.

Will you write me immediately? Write me. When I receive your letters I feel as though they're fanning me with peacock feathers.

Last night my brother and I serenaded Falla. What an amusing thing! I arranged the "Song of the Phantom Fire" for trombone, clarinet, tuba and cornet.[4] I assure you it was a devilish thing . . . and marvelous! Four musicians from the municipal band took charge of playing it and it was a delightful surprise for Manolo and María del Carmen.[5] They laughed so much they couldn't get up to open the door for us . . . , but here comes the funny part: Falla said that that instrumentation was a work of genius, and that even the great Don Igor [Stravinsky] never dreamed of it; and yelling and shouting he took the four ragged musicians into his room and made them repeat the laughable noise four times accompanying them on the piano! I tell you I really enjoyed it immensely. Well and good . . . , since this morning he comes to my house and tells me that the idea I had of doing a puppet theater must be carried to conclusion, and he tells me to entreat you to finish the Cristóbal, which I see now as the first episode of the puppet show. Falla is pledged to do the music like that last night (!) for other things, and assures me that Don Igor and Ravel would immediately do *something* with it. Manuelito thinks, if we do this, of touring Europe and America with our puppet theater which would be called: The Billy Club Puppets of Granada. So you see, Adolfito, how the mess of last night served some purpose after all. Falla is so enthusiastic that last night he couldn't sleep thinking of the instrumentation he'd do for the Punch character, and I draw your attention to this so you'd get on with our Cristóbal, which will be the first we present in the inauguration of the Spanish puppets. I'm also very happy, because, if we do ˊthis, I'll go with you, Adolfito, into something which has been the dream of my youth. I'm very eager to talk with you in order to begin the work in earnest.

Now I'm going to gather up my family and go up to the Maestro's house, since it's his day and there's a *big bash* in his garden. *Adiós,* Adolfito, with a small letter a. A tender embrace from

Federico

Regards from Paquito [García Lorca] and Alfonso [García Valdecasas].

Your hieroglyphics are very good!!!

Don't tell anyone, but how poor Gerardo Diego's stuff is. What a pauper with images!

---

[1] Play on words, referring to Salazar's role in the project.

[2] Variations on the Andalusian *Cante Jondo* (deep song).

[3] Play on the word *Indice* (meaning *Index*), the magazine which served as a focal point and stimulus for the young poets of the "Generation of '27" from 1921–24. The editor, poet Juan Ramón Jiménez (1881–1958), received the Nobel Prize for literature in 1956.

[4] Manuel de Falla's *"Canción del fuego fátuo"* from *"El amor brujo"* (1916).

[5] The composer's sister.

TO REGINO SAINZ DE LA MAZA

[Granada, 1922]

Dear Regino:

I'm a scoundrel for not having answered you sooner, but my work and my *special* situation and state of mind held me back. Forgive me, but you know very well that this poor poet and hardened dreamer loves you a lot although not as much as you deserve. This year I haven't gone back to Madrid because I've been doing *things* that I haven't been able to carry through in the Town of the Bear [Madrid] because of their Andalusian ways and their special rhythm. And now I'm glad, since I've finished a poem that seemed unattainable, and besides Falla and I are projecting *great things* that you'll see by and by. I'm happy. Granada has given me new visions and has filled my (too tender) heart with unforeseen things. I want to see you so much!! Why don't you come? Make up your mind!

My book has been very successful. Jean Aubry is going to translate many of the poems into French and a few days ago I received articles written about it from London and Milan. Isn't that delightful? . . . But I'm lost . . . poetry has become master of my soul. Like any Joe Blow, I'm locked in a cage of metaphors. I can't send you the *Book of Poems* because I don't even have one copy; if I leave soon for Madrid I'll give you a copy there if any remain. I think of you constantly and I love you *a whole lot*. Write me right away at greater length, and I promise to answer.

Federico

If you see Roberto Gerahar (I don't know how it's spelled) give him a hug.

MANUEL DE FALLA

[Asquerosa, July or August, 1922]

Dear Don Manué (colon)

I'm enthusiastic about the projected trip to La Alpujarra. You already know how I dream of producing some *puppet shows* full of Andalusian emotion and exquisite popular sentiment.

I believe we should do this very seriously; the Billy Club Puppets lend themselves to the creation of very original songs.

We should do the tragedy (never praised enough) of the gentlemen of the flute and the mosquito with the golden trumpet, the savage idyll of Don Cristóbal and the *Miss* Rosita, the death of Pepe-Hillo in the plaza of Madrid and some other farces of our own invention. Then we'll have to do crime ballads and that miracle of the Virgen del Carmen where the fish and the waves of the sea speak. If we go to La Alpujarra we should bring along some Moorish topic like that of Aben-Humeya. If we put a little love into this work we'll be able to produce a clean and faultless *art,* not "aht."

Will you be dropping by one of these days? There was a character with some puppets in town a few days ago who *involved* the whole crowd in a truly Aristophanic way.

Manolito [Angeles Ortiz] and you can do delightful things and [José] Mora [Guarnido], who really knows the popular ballad, can be very helpful. I'm ready for anything, as you very well know, except sending telegrams!

On behalf of my father, thanks for your greeting. Regards and *all the best* from my mother and sister to María del Carmen [Falla], and here goes a strong and devoted hug from your friend always

Federico

Come visit!

TO MELCHOR FERNANDEZ ALMAGRO

[Granada, 1922]

Dear Melchorito:

Probably around the 22nd I'll be there for that [?]; I'll let you know. What do you think? Before going [to Madrid] I'm going to give a lecture on the *Cante Jondo*,[1] which I believe will be very interesting and immediately afterwards I'll leave. I remember you constantly and we speak a lot about you, Manolito [Manuel Angeles Ortiz] and I. Poor Manolo! Now he's calmer, but he was in a bad way, because it was all memories.

I ardently desire to be in the Capital although I find the actual literary atmosphere terribly nauseating. I feel far removed from the present poetic rot and I dream of a future dawn that contains the ineffable emotion of pristine skies. I feel like an Equator between the orange and the lemon.

I love the clear water and the turbid star.

You'll come to meet me. If you could see how troubled I've been this past season!

With love as always.

Federico

Will you come to meet me?

Hugs from Paquito. Best regards to Pizarrín [Miguel Pizarro Zambrano]. Tell him I love him.

---

[1] Thirteen of Lorca's lectures, essays, and other prose pieces including "Deep Song" (*Cante Jondo*) are collected, in English translation, in *Deep Song and Other Prose*, edited and translated by Christopher Maurer, New York, 1980.

TO REGINO SAINZ DE LA MAZA

[Granada, 1922]

[Granada. —Acera del Casino, 31, in case you forgot.]

Dear Regino:

I received your letter in Madrid moments before returning to this marvelous city, and now I'm answering you begging you insistently not to delay as much in answering me. I'm crazy with happiness over a number of things that I'll tell you about when we see each other (and may it be soon) and that give my life a high artistic meaning, a true and pure spiritual meaning.

I'm suffering now from *truly* lyrical *attacks* and work like a child putting together a crèche; such is my illusion.

I remember you with so much happiness and I long to hear you. Have you made progress? Study a lot, Regino, and comb with care the invisible strands of your heart. Be careful not to tangle them! I've spoken of you and proposed to my friends that you give concerts in a salon of independents which we are organizing and where I will give lectures. It's a stupendous thing! You will play only primitive music, since I believe it has the most character alongside [Rafael] Barradas' pictures, etc., etc. You'll be amazed by the plans! I want to keep up your curiosity so that it will scratch your lyrical soul, disturbed today by the Catalan mud, that soul of yours with six string glances.

Curiosity has a cat's claws (didn't you know that, Regino?). Sharp little claws that scratch the walls of the breast and make Madame Distraction close her one hundred vertiginous and cursed eyes. . . . That's why I'm igniting that fantasy in you.

If you could only see! I have such enthusiasm . . . ! My hands are full of dead kisses (apples of snow, with the trembling furrow of lips) and I hope to throw them into the broken air in order to catch newer ones. Answer me immediately. A cordial embrace.

Federico

Vela has died. I don't wish to comment on it. Today Angel Barrios gave me regards for you. [Manuel de] Falla is here and I'm up to here listening to his things. What a marvel! We three are planning a trip to the Alpujarra. I am going to Madrid on the 8th (and you?).

TO MELCHOR FERNANDEZ ALMAGRO

[Granada, end of December, 1922]

Dear Melchor:

It's been some time since I've written just *to you alone,* without anyone's collaboration, and I don't want to let time pass without congratulating you on your succinct first article for *Sur.* [José] Mora [Guarnido] is still the man of long articles, and what happened concerning that letter was that he would have wanted you to let loose with everything you've got, sending twenty pages, but we're all enthusiastic about your things, you know that already . . . and Mora most of all! We'll see about it when it comes out; although they're enthusiastic, they don't care much for work.

The *object* of *this letter* is to invite you to the puppet show that [Manuel de] Falla and I are going to give in my house. It will be an extraordinary puppet show and we will produce something of pure art, which we need so badly. In *Cristobicas* we will perform a poem full of tenderness and grotesque turns that I've composed with music arranged by Falla for clarinet, viola and piano. The poem is called "The Child Who Waters the Basil and the Nosy Prince" and has a great Granadan flavor. We will also stage, with the same set up as *Cristobicas,* the brief play by Cervantes, *The Talkers,* with music by Stravinsky. And to conclude we will perform, in a theatrical way, the old *Play of the Three Wise Men,* with fifteenth-century music and decorations copied from the codex of Albert the Great in our University.

Will you come, Melchorito? Get a move on and help us with this party for Isabelita's playmates.

We're all very happy. Falla saying: "Oh, it's going to be a special thing!" seems like a little boy. Last night he stayed up late working and writing out the instrumental parts with a boy's enthusiasm.

You should come!

Adiós, Melchor. A hug from this little poet.

Federico

How wonderful Granada is at Easter time!
Do you remember? . . . Then come.

TO MELCHOR FERNANDEZ ALMAGRO

[Granada, Spring, 1922 or 1923]

Dear Melchorito:

I'm going to the country. I'd like for us to correspond this summer and you could keep me *completely up to date* with everything that happens over there. I'm very happy, but overwrought,
I don't know why. . . . Every morning I feel an irresistible urge
to cry all alone with a soft and happy weeping; that's right,
happy! Anything moves me (the emotion of dawn). . . . It seems
to me as though I'm recuperating from some sickness and I'm as
tired as if I had crossed deserts swollen with fever. I'm thinking
now of doing a lot of work beneath my eternal poplars and "beneath the pianissimo of gold." I'd like to produce a calm and
serene work this summer; I'm thinking of constructing various
ballads with lagoons, ballads with mountains, ballads with stars;
a mysterious and clear work, that would be like a flower (arbitrary and perfect as a flower): all perfume! I'd like to extract
from the shadows the Arab girls who played in these towns and
to lose in my lyrical groves the ideal figures of anonymous ballads. Imagine a ballad with *skies* instead of lagoons. Nothing
could be more exciting! This summer, if God helps me with his
little doves, I will produce a popular and very Andalusian work.
I'm going to travel a little through these marvelous towns, whose
castles, whose people never existed, it seems, for poets and. . . .
Enough of Castile!!

Tonight all the people in the Little Corner group are getting
together to eat at *el último*,[1] and there will be sensational news,
which we'll be passing on to you, since we think you can help a
lot. Of course, we're thinking of naming you consul general of
the Little Corner group in Madrid. The idea that will be put
forth for consideration tonight at the banquet (I can't resist it)
is the following. . . . But don't speak to anybody about her [the
idea] until she's engaged, because someone might grab her, and
that wouldn't be good. It's a question, dear Melchor, of building
a Mohammedan hermitage on the grounds [Francisco] Soriano
[Lapresa] is offering us on his ranch of Zubia in honor of Abentofail[2] and two or three more geniuses of Granadan Arabic culture.

In it there would be a library of Granadan Arabic things, and outside would be planted, around the monument, willows, palm trees and cypresses. What joy, Melchorito, to see the white cupola of the hermitage from the Puerta Real and the little tower accompanying it! Besides it would be the first memorial we've had in Spain for these sublime men, Granadans of pure stock, who today pervade the world of Islam. [José] Navarro [Pardo] almost cried for joy last night, and [Antonio Alvarez de] Cienfuegos, [Francisco] Campos [Aravaca] and everyone else are all crazy about the idea. It would be a private thing *carried out by our Little Corner group,* which would acquire great renown this way, right? We're hoping that our friends in Madrid will help out with enthusiasm. We're also thinking of inviting Moorish scholars from the East, who would come to Granada, and of doing an anthology of Abentofail edited by Navarro, with my things which I'll do when the time comes. Soriano was the first contributor with a thousand *pesetas.* We think that the cupola of the hermitage should be spangled with stars, like that of the baths, and Manolo [Angeles] Ortiz will decorate the interior with hieratic themes and Oriental motifs. How does it strike you? To-night is a great night for all of us. We will toast you and Juan Cristóbal, who doesn't seem to like us, though we like him a lot, and we will give a cheer for the Little Corner. Don't say anything to anyone until we notify you *officially.*

Adiós. A very big hug from

Federico (the perfidious)

(Give regards and a little kiss on each cheek to the Apollonian Pepito de Ciria y Escalante, shameless with his friends and a rascal.)

---

[1] According to Manuel Montesinos: "*El último* was the unofficial name of exactly that, 'the last' place where one could get something to eat on the road that went, and still goes, from Granada to the mountains. It was called *el último ventorillo.* And even though it no longer is last, it still retains the name."

[2] Abentofail: twelfth-century physician and philosopher, born in Cádiz, author of *Hayy ibn Yaqzan (Alive, son of Awake).*

[Granada, Summer, 1923]

Dear Melchor:

(Pardon the paper!)

I'm in Granada, where it's really hellishly hot (odd, isn't it? But I'm used to the country! . . .)

I came to meet my friends and to talk over a delightful matter with Falla. It's about the *Billy Club Puppets* I'm *fabricating,* in which the maestro will have an active part. I'll tell you about it . . . if you answer me immediately. I see you aren't writing me; I've written you two long letters, and you, in exchange, one and not very long at that.

I'm working rather hard. I've *composed* a couple of poems about the cuckoo (admirable and symbolic little bird) and the *daydreams of a river,* little plaintive poems that I feel inside, in the deepest part of my unhappy heart. You have no idea how much I suffer when I see myself portrayed in these poems; I imagine that I'm an immense violet colored mosquito on the backwater of emotion. Stitch and stitch . . . like a shoemaker, stitch, stitching away, and nothing to show! These days I feel pregnant. *I have seen* an admirable book that someone must do and I would like it to be me. It is "The Meditations and Allegories of Water." What deep and striking marvels can be told about water! The water poem in my book has opened up inside my soul. I see a great poem of the water, somewhere between the Oriental and Christian, European; a poem where one could sing in ample verses or in prose, *molto rubato,* the impassioned life and martyrdoms of water. A great Life of Water, with very detailed analysis of the concentric circle of reflection, of the drunken music unmixed with the silence created by the currents. The river and the water courses have penetrated me. Now one must say: the Guadalquivir or the Miño are born in Fuente Miña and flow into Federico García Lorca, modest dreamer and son of the water. I should like God to grant me strength and joy enough. Oh, yes, joy (!) to write the book I visualize, this book of devotion for those who travel through the desert. Although you would call me the Seco de Lucena[1] of the Sahara!

I even visualize the chapters and the stanzas (there will be prose and verse), for example:

The "Looms of Water," "Map of Water," "The Shallows of Sounds," "Meditation of the Spring," "The Still Water." And later, when it touches . . . yes, touches! (pray to the saints to give me happiness) on dead water, what a stirring poem, that of the Alhambra seen as a pantheon of water!

I believe that if I attacked this boldly I'd be able to do something, and if I were a great poet, what one calls a great poet, I might find myself face to face with my great poem.

In short, Melchorcito, you know that you're maybe one of the three people to whom I'm telling this; I know that you love me and, most of all, you *enliven* me in a way for which I can't thank you enough.

Tomorrow I'm going to the country. Write me immediately and tell me a lot about everything.

A strong hug from this guy (with his little peter and everything),

Federico

From a little poem ("Daydreams of the River"), a stone from the edifice I'm thinking about.

SLOW CURRENT

> Down the river go my eyes,
> down the river . . .
> Down the river goes my love,
> down the river . . .
> (My heart goes on counting
> the hours it's been sleeping.)
> The river carries dry leaves,
> the river . . .
> The river is clear and deep,
> the river . . .
> (My heart asks me
> if it can change places.)

(Oh what a water obsession I suffer!) *Adiós.*

---

[1] Luis Seco de Lucena: editor of the newspaper, *El Defensor de Granada,* and author of a guide to the city.

[Asquerosa, July, 1923]

Dear Pepito and Melchorito:

In truth I am *widowed* without you two.

I would like the three of us to be the holy trinity of Friendship. A poet (don't laugh, Melchor) and three realities. Are you working, Ciria? You're incorrigible! And you, Melchor, anguished and pathetic, what are you doing facing the sea?

You've no idea how I love and remember you.

I've finished a poem: "The Garden of the Moon's Grapefruit," and I'm ready to work the whole summer on it, since I have an infinite illusion that it should be the way I've seen it. One can say that I've done it in a feverish manner, since I've worked twenty days and twenty nights, but it has only been *to pin it down*. The landscapes in this poem are absolutely still, without any wind or motion at all. I noticed that my verses were slipping through my fingers, that my actual poem is ecstatic and somnambulistic. My *garden* is the garden of possibilities, the garden of what is not, but could (and at times) should have been; the garden of theories that passed away without having been seen and of children who haven't been born. Each word of the poem was a butterfly and one by one I had to catch them.

Then I sustained a struggle with my two secular enemies (and those of all poets) Eloquence and Common Sense. . . . The frightening struggle of hand to hand combat, as in the battles of the *Poem of the Cid*.

If you're good friends of mine, write me right away, right away, and I'll send you a song from that garden; for example, the "Song of the Boy with Seven Hearts" or the "Lament of the Voiceless Girl," that seem to me sufficiently *accomplished*.

I didn't write to Gerardo Diego to thank him for sending me his beautiful book *Soria*. . . . But you know, Melchorito, that when I'm not close to the person to whom I'm writing, I don't know what to say to him! And although Diego's book is good and he's a great poet, it was work to thank him, praise him, and that's all! . . . I'm a man overboard! *I'm not worldly* and the whole *world* will be displeased with me. But I can't help it! If you see Gerardo tell him how much I admire him and shake his hand on my behalf.

Pepito, work, for God's sake, and answer me immediately!

Yours

Federico

I am in the country. My address:

San Pascual.

(Apeadero.)

Granada.

I'll cable you the money I owe you, Melchor. Forgive me!

[Asquerosa, July, 1923]

[Drawing: earthen jar]

Dear Melchorito:

I haven't written before because you had no right to delay answering me the way you did, knowing how I value your letters.

My season in the country is coming to an end, and within a few days we'll be returning to Granada, and from there probably to Málaga (the city I love most of all in Andalusia, for its marvelous and stirring flesh and blood sensuality), where I'll see the sea, the only force that torments and disturbs me in Nature. . . . More than the sky! Much more!

At this very moment I could begin to tell you so much about the sea . . . but only that the sea might hear it! Before the sea I forget my sex, my condition, my soul, my gift of tears . . . everything! But my heart is pierced by a sharp desire to imitate it, bitter, phosphoric and eternally awake.

It's curious that I don't envy or desire the things of man, but only the thingness of Things. . . . But if I go on this way, I'm going to bore you, and I don't want to. . . . There are certain sentiments that shouldn't be displayed . . . and I have papers to prove it (I really do)!

I've worked rather hard and I'm finishing up a series of *gypsy ballads* which I like wholeheartedly. I'm also doing modern interpretations of figures from Greek mythology, a new thing for me that I find very amusing. As for theater I've finished the first act of a comedy (in the style of the Billy Club Puppets) that is called *The Shoemaker's Prodigious Wife,* where no more is said than the bare minimum and everything else is insinuated. Since I believe one can tell if a play is good or bad just by reading the cast of characters, I'm sending it to you so you can tell me what you think.

1. The shoemaker's wife.
2. The neighbor dressed in red.
3. The old lady.
4. The shoemaker.
5. Don Mirlo.

6. The boy Amargo.
7. The boy Alcalde.
8. Tatachín's uncle.
   Neighbors and priests.

MUSIC:
Flute and guitar.

Read the cast of characters to Cipriano [Rivas Cherif], the *charming* and *intelligent* playwright, and ask him if he wishes to collaborate with me on another thing I'm preparing, which I'll tell him about.

Adiós, Melchorito. Regards to all and a hug for you from

Federico

Give [Enrique Díez-] Canedo a hug if he's there. Soon I'll send you *that,*[1] within a day or two of going to Granada.

I'm sending you poems to look over.

[1] Lorca is probably referring to money.

TO JOSE DE CIRIA Y ESCALANTE

[Asquerosa, July 30, 1923]

How good lemons look on the
breasts of an opulent woman!

[Drawing: four lemons]

Dear Pepito:

After a long auto trip I found your postcard a few days late and I
thank you very much for praising my poems which you still don't
know.

I'm spending a feverish and bitter summer, pestered by a
crowd of poems that make my life impossible. That's why I've
decided to dedicate my attention to my "Garden of the Moon's
Grapefruit" and leave the others for later. Yesterday the old
shepherdess Amarilis visited me, coming out of the geometric
night of sonnets for me to sing to her, old and trembling, crowned
by rag flowers. She came from visiting the *ultraístas;*[1] but since
they were with Eve, futurist Eve, well, naturally, they didn't pay
any attention to her. . . . And it seemed such a shame to me!
. . . I treated her very well; I gave her a cup of coffee with milk
and I promised to resurrect her in a poem in which she would
go singing, covered by cicadas and fireflies, through a field of
narcissus and crystals. If she visits you and [Gerardo] Diego, do
right by her; you should know that she is very old and can die
on us at any moment. I beg you to do this poem of old Amarilis
so I can finish and *polish* my very strange garden of moon grape-
fruits.

I'm going to send you various drafts of this poem, on the condition that you don't read them to anybody, since they are not
yet finished. You promise?

Now more than ever words seem to me to be illuminated by a
phosphorescent light and full of mysterious sounds and mean-
ings. I feel a real panic when it comes to writing! . . . And what
great pleasure our old poets give me! . . . Pepito, tell me by
return mail what you think about my poor verses. But don't
read them to anyone! Each day I suffer more seeing that I have
to publish my *Suites* soon.

In September Falla and I will prepare the second presentation of the Billy Club Puppets, in which we'll put on a witches' tale with *infernal music* by Falla, and Ernesto Halffter and Adolfito Salazar will also collaborate. Give affectionate greetings on my behalf to our comrade Gerardo Diego.

Don't read my verses to anyone!

And write me right away, sending me your things.

Adiós. Your poet

Federico

If after sending you so many things you don't answer right away, telling me clearly what you think about them, I'll get mad and I won't dedicate anything to you.

Here go these poems:

[*"Portico," "Cancioncilla del niño que no nació"* ("Little Song of the Unborn Child"), *"El sátiro blanco"* ("The White Satyr"), *"Arco de lunas"* ("Moon Haloes"), *"Otra estampita"* ("Another Small Sketch"), *"Tierra/Cielo"* ("Earth/Sky"), *"Amanecer y re-pique"* ("Dawn and Bell-toll").]

[1] Ultraism: post World War I literary movement based on the use of extravagant image and metaphor.

42

TO MANUEL DE FALLA

[Asquerosa, August, 1923]

Dear Don Manuel!:

Is the ceramic [dedicatory] plaque for Glinka coming along at last?[1]

I would like to have affirmative news regarding this matter which is so right and proper; I for one am inclined to *go all out* in order to get it done. (Answer *yes* or *no,* as Christ teaches us.)

You can't imagine how I recall you when I play the guitar and wish *to pluck out* by force (!) your marvelous *Homage to Debussy,* of which I can't get more than the first notes. It's truly elegant! And my mother despairs and hides the guitar in the most remote corner of the house. Have you thought much about *our* thing? I think we should settle the darned trio and the finale so you can get to work in peace.

I've received a letter from a futurist poet, Adriano del Valle, and he instructs me to greet you, calling you "Falla, that sigh of Boabdil transmuted into music,"[2] very funny, isn't it. For my part tell María del Carmen that she is the "sigh of Queen Zalima transmuted into *repoussé*" so she won't be displeased.

Regards from my whole family, greetings to your sister and you know how you are loved by your very devoted poet

Federico

I'm arranging for publication of the *Poem of the Cante Jondo.* And if you're considering the matter of Glinka and Murciano, be sure to notify me right away.

---

[1] The Russian composer Mikhail Glinka (1804–1857) visited Granada in 1845, accompanied by the celebrated guitarist Francisco Rodríguez Murciano.

[2] Boabdil (d. 1538) was the last King of the Moorish Kingdom of Granada. Legend recalls his farewell sigh when, on his way into exile, he looked back at the city for the last time.

[Asquerosa, September, 1923]

Dear Melchorito:

Marianita, in her house in Granada, ponders whether or not she should sew the flag of Liberty. Through the street walks a man selling "fine lavender from the *sierra*" and another "oranges, little oranges of Almería," and the recently planted trees of the small plaza of La Gracia already know, from the birds and the pine tree in the seminary, that a tragic ballad full of color will put them to sleep in the nights of the full turquoise moon of the plain. If you could only see what deep emotion trembles in my eyes in the presence of the *legendary Marianita*! . . . Since childhood I've been hearing these lines, so very suggestive:

> Marianita went out for a walk
> and a soldier stepped out to meet her . . .

Dressed in white, with her hair loose and a melodramatic expression verging on the sublime, this woman has strolled through the secret little road of my childhood with an unmistakable air. A woman half seen and loved at the age of nine, when I went from Fuente Vaqueros to Granada in an old stagecoach, whose driver played a wild tune on his copper trumpet. If I'm afraid of doing this play, it's precisely because I'm *disturbing* my very delicate memories of that martyred blonde widow.

What do you advise? I'd like to do a *processional* drama . . . , a *simple* and *hieratic* narrative, amidst evocations and mysterious breezes like an old Madonna with her arch of cherubs. A kind of blind man's *stylized* [broadside] ballad. A crime, in short, where the red of the blood mixes with the red of the curtains. Mariana, according to the ballad and according to the slight history that surrounds her, is a woman passionate in the extreme, a woman *possessed,* a case of the magnificent love of an Andalusian woman in an extremely *political* atmosphere (I don't know if I'm explaining myself well). She gives herself to love for love's sake, while the others are obsessed by Liberty. She ends up a martyr of Liberty, being in reality (even history seems to bear this out) a *victim* of her own enamored and maddened heart.

She's a Juliet without Romeo and she's closer to the madrigal than the ode. When she decides to die, she's already dead, and death doesn't frighten her in the least. In the last act she will be dressed in white and all the decor will be in the same tone. Neither the ballad nor history prevent me at all from imagining it thus. . . . What's more: my mother has told me that these things are whispered about in Granada. I would like you to know the plot and the scene divisions. Write me immediately. Tomorrow I'm leaving for Granada. Send your letters there.

I saw what [Eugenio] d'Ors says about me. Very funny!

Adiós. A hug from your poet and true friend

Federico

Answer me at length.
I'll wire you from Granada.

TO MELCHOR FERNANDEZ ALMAGRO

[Granada, October, 1923]

Dear Melchor:

I am in the midst of agreeable and disagreeable literary *tasks*. I work nearly all day on the poetic[1] work I'm doing with Falla and I think it will soon be finished so I can go on with my *Marianita*. I'd like to publish my *Suites,* but I'm at the point where *I can't do any more*. Write me about everything. I also want to finish my poem "The Game of the Mad Child and the Bird without a Nest." . . . In short—there's so much to do!

I am grateful for your article.[2] You can't imagine how much!

The "Suite of the Return" is long, but I'm sending you its most delicate little bangles.

> I return
> for my wings.
> Let me return!
> I want to die being
> the dawn.
> I want to die being
> yesterday!
> I return
> for my wings.
> Let me return!
> I want to die being
> a fountain.
> I want to die outside
> the sea.[3]
> I want to return to infancy,
> and from infancy, to shadow.
> > Are you leaving, nightingale?
> > Then go.
> I want to return to the shadow,
> and from the shadow, to the flower.
> > Are you leaving, sweet scent?
> > Then go.

I'd like to return to the flower,
and from the flower,
to my heart.

Federico

[1] A little opera, with music by Falla.

[2] Article titled *"El mundo lírico de García Lorca"* ("The Lyrical World of García Lorca") published in *España*, October 13, 1923.

[3] Appears with variation in the play *Así que pasen cinco años* (*When Five Years Pass*).

TO ANTONIO GALLEGO BURIN

[Asquerosa, Spring, 1924?]

Dear Antonio:

After such a long silence, today I send you a little string of words. It's true that I don't write to anybody, but I know you will all forgive me, because at heart you know I love you as always.

It's a bit tiresome of me to ask you to do a big favor. . . . But to whom shall I turn if not you?

My project is to produce a great theatrical ballad based on Marianita Pineda and I have already resolved it, to the joy of Gregorio [Martínez Sierra] and Catalina [Bárcena], who see the possibilities of *something strong*. My idea is to stage the last days of that Granadan woman.

I know that you have devoted a lot of time to studying this figure (of course in another way), and I should like you to give me information on her in order to create a little atmosphere.

My characters are, besides her, Pedrosa, Sotomayor and the nuns of the Recogidas [convent]. What I've thought up is something new, and I'm happy. I think it will be ready to premier this coming year. Please keep it absolutely quiet. You know what happens with these things.

Melchorito [Melchor Fernández Almagro], who's enchanted with my idea, has given me interesting notes but I believe that you are the one who can give me facts on this topic.

Antonio, if it happens that you are thinking of doing something with Mariana, I don't want to interfere in the matter; besides these are very different things. I just want a biography of her and some facts about the conspiracy. As you can understand, the dramatic interest lies in the character I want to create and in the tale, which has nothing to do with the historical, because I've invented it myself. I'd like you to guide me with reference to Pedrosa and to tell me where I could find out about the state of Granada in that epoch.

I have enough to go on with a few *notes*. What's essential is already thought out. . . . But I don't want *to put my foot in it*, do you understand?

Antonio, you don't know with what joy I look forward to your letter, since I really want to get to work.

Regards to Eloísa [Morell Márquez], kisses to the little one and a big hug from your friend who asks too many questions

Federico (*pico*)[1]

---

[1] *Pico* means "beak"—someone who is always asking favors.

TO MELCHOR FERNANDEZ ALMAGRO

[Asquerosa, end of July, 1924]

Dear Melchorito:

We're in the country now, after having spent a few days in Granada accompanied by Juan Ramón [Jiménez] and Zenobia. They were truly amazed and satisfied by Granada. Juan Ramón has said very perceptive things about the city and has forged a great friendship with my family, since he spent whole days at my house. Most of all he was enthusiastic about my sister, little Isabel, to whom he's already written a letter from Moguer.[1]

Zenobia was very pleased, poor dear, to see the melancholy poet so happy.

Juan Ramón told me that he has the need to be in constant touch with me in Madrid and he sent me sad and indirect complaints about my attitude with respect to him, and he's right!

Now that I've dealt with him intimately I've been able to observe what a profound sensitivity and what a divine quantity of poetry his soul possesses. One day he told me: "We'll go to the Generalife at five o'clock in the afternoon, the hour in which the gardens begin to *suffer*." This is a full-length portrait of him, right? And seeing the stair of water he said: "In autumn, if I'm here, I'll die." And he said this with the utmost conviction. We spoke a long time about the fairies and I restrained myself quite well from showing him the little water sprites, since that would have been too much for him. I'll be telling you other things later—the moving discoveries I've made in the fantasy world of Granada.

I've been having a nightmare about Pepe Ciria.[2] I remember him more with each passing day. What a tragic friend! And how hard it is to forget him! But I can tell you in secret that he hasn't died . . . I don't know why . . . , but I don't have the slightest doubt that he has not died.

Melchor, answer me immediately. Tell me all about Madrid and our mutual friends, Claudio's banquet,[3] everything.

Regards to your dear family.
A hug.

Federico

I'm in the country, remember?
Apeadero de San Pascual.

[1] The letter to Isabel García Lorca, dated July 19, 1924, was published in the *Cartas de Juan Ramón Jiménez* edited by Francisco Garfias, Madrid, 1962.

[2] The poet José de Ciria y Escalante died on June 4, 1924. Lorca, Juan Ramón Jiménez, and Melchor Fernández Almagro visited his tomb in the cemetery of Madrid on June 19, 1924.

[3] Claudio de la Torre: playwright.

TO MELCHOR FERNANDEZ ALMAGRO

[Granada, August, 1924]

Dear Melchorito:

Your letter took so long! . . . But better late than never. Did you like Burgos? What a sweet memory, full of truth and tears, overcomes me when I think of Burgos. . . . Does this shock you? I am nourished by Burgos, because the cathedral's great towers of air and silver showed me the *narrow gate* through which I had to pass in order to know myself and know my soul. What green poplars! What an old wind! Oh, Tower of Gamonal and Sepulcher on San Amaro! And, oh, my child heart! . . . My heart never again will be as alive, as full of pain and eternal grace.

Your card from Burgos has exacerbated my old painful stigmata and has caused a resin of light and nostalgia to well from my body.

I piously remember [Martín Domínguez] Berrueta (who treated me in such a charming way) since it was through him that I lived unforgettable hours which made a profound impression on my life as a poet.

But I have no time now to ask him to forgive me . . . , although he smiles at me from afar. . . . God will have forgiven him his childish pedantry and his petty pride in exchange for his enthusiasm, which, even if it were (and this is not known) for *ulterior motives,* was, in the end, *enthusiasm,* the wing of the holy spirit.

I've had a bad time these past few days, because I wanted to dedicate to our friend [José de] Ciria [y Escalante] a tender and authentic memorial, but no matter how hard I struggled I couldn't get (and this is rare for me) my fountain, my fountain!, to flow for him. Yesterday afternoon I was in a cool and dark poplar grove and I told him: "Pepe, why don't you want me to evoke you?" And I felt my eyes fill with tears. Then, after ten days of continuous effort, I was able to give birth in an instant to the sonnet I'm sending you.

But it seems to me that we should *commune* through Ciria and forget him in appearance. One must *make him a part of oneself* and smile without knowing his name. Do you always keep in mind that you have eyes? And, nevertheless, all of life enters us through them. Let us convert our dead into *our blood* and forget them.

Once in a while I'm seized by a strange happiness I have never felt before. The very sad happiness of being a poet! And nothing matters to me. Not even death!

If you answer me immediately, I will send you poems and drawings. In a few days, the angelic Falla will get to work on my little opera. I expect we'll have a good time, since the subject has wit and style, which is necessary in any theatrical poem.

Adiós. Write me soon. A hug for you and best regards to your family.

Federico

ON THE DEATH OF JOSE DE CIRIA Y ESCALANTE

Who can say that he saw you? And at what moment?
What sorrow of illuminated shadow!
Two voices resound: the clock and the wind.
While dawn floats off without you.
A delirium of ashen spikenards
invades your delicate brow.
Man! Passion! Sorrow of light! Memento.
Return turned into moon and heart of nothing!
Return turned into moon: With my own hand
I'll toss your apple over the turbid river
of red fish in summer.
And you, above, on high, green and cold,
forget yourself!, and forget the vain world,
delicate Giocondo. My friend!

This sonnet, naturally, contains a lot of restrained and static sentiment. I'm satisfied. Although I'll have to polish it a bit. Is it worthy of Ciria? Tell me the truth. I'd like to dedicate three or four to him and I want them to be sonnets, because the sonnet preserves an eternal sentiment, which doesn't fit in any other vessel better than this apparently cold one. Tell me what you think of this.

Adiós, and console yourself thinking how our friend is with God in the divine surroundings of air and endless sky. Death to cold science! Long live mystic science, and love, and friendship!

TO MELCHOR FERNANDEZ ALMAGRO

[Granada, September, 1924]

Dear Melchorito:

I'm in Granada where I got your letter. You don't know how pleased I am that you like my poems, most of all the gypsy ballad. If you answer me soon, I'll send you a *somnambulistic ballad* I've finished. I like Granada to the point of delirium, but in order to live differently; to live in a *carmen*,[1] and the rest is foolishness; to live near what one loves and feels: whitewashed wall, myrtle, and fountain.

I'm a bit sad because I'm separated from all of you, from you in particular and from Pepín [José Bello]. Your letters are my happiness. Here, in Granada, I no longer have friends. Everybody's new and they look at me in the Alhambra as if I'm a slightly mad outsider, who goes round and round the infinite patio of Lindaraja not wanting to find the exit (which it shouldn't have).

We don't know where to go, because my father has bad nerves and lives very sadly, believing that he's going to die from one moment to the next, without having any physical disability, a thing which, as is natural, makes us ill at ease and ill-humored.

Tomorrow I'll start working seriously, although with each passing day I wish I hadn't written anything and could start with a clean slate of rhyme and rhythm.

Answer me quickly!

Federico

["*Canción del Arbolé*" ("Song of the Tree") was enclosed plus three other short poems, later titled "*Es verdad*" ("It is True"), "*Canción cantada*" ("Song Sung"), and "*Al oído de una muchacha*" ("To a Girl's Ear").]

[1] Villa and garden within a walled enclosure.

54

TO MELCHOR FERNANDEZ ALMAGRO

[Granada, Autumn, 1924]

And then what? For how long has the prince been putting Cinderella's shoe on?[1] The day he gets up from his cushion the world will come to an end.

What's the furthest corner? Because that's where I want to be, alone with the only thing that I love.

My poetry is a game.

My life is a game.

But I am not a game.

The world is a shoulder of dark meat (black flesh of an old mule). And the light is on the other side.

I'd like to be naked as a zero and *contemplate*.

I feel like taking a long trip somewhere. But never to foolish and mysterious Japan nor to dirty India recently awakened for all time. I'd like to travel through Europe, where one takes out the coin to throw to the bottom of love.

Are you Melchorito? Yes? I didn't know that. I don't have a single friend. But this fills me with satisfaction.

Right now I have no projects . . . yes! . . . But I work intensely. I've put together a book of dialogues and one of poetry. A small natural history, a garland of fruit with insects crawling in it.

And now I'm preparing a grotesque theatrical work:

The Love of Don Perlimplín
with Belisa in the Garden.[2]

They're the "Hallelujahs" I told you about at the Savoy [café]. Do you remember? I take an idiot's delight in this. You have no idea.

But then these things are poor. But didn't you know that? Very poor. If I had faith in them . . . I'd be singing another tune . . . because today I could go off to Italy, which is my dream, and I can't because my parents are angry with me.

As soon as I finish this work I'll see about earning a living. If I can do it, I'm thinking about taking some sort of qualifying exams, and if not . . . we'll see! I don't think money will be a problem as long as I'm strong.

Life is very *intense* for me right now.

I'll always be happy if they'd leave me alone in that delightful and unknown furthest corner, apart from struggles, putrefactions and nonsense; the ultimate corner of sugar and toast, where the mermaids catch the branches of the willows and the heart opens to a flute's sharpness. Granada is horrible. This is not Andalusia. Andalusia is something else. It's in the people. And here they're Gallicians.

I, who am an Andalusian and an Andalusian through and through, sigh for Málaga, for Córdoba, for Sanlúcar la Mayor, for Algeciras, for authentic and high-toned Cádiz, for Alcalá de los Gazules, for that which is *intimately* Andalusian. The real Granada has vanished, and now appears dead beneath greenish and delirious gas lights. The other Andalusia is alive; for example: Málaga.

Adiós, Melchorito. Since I know you don't like me, don't bother answering, because it would trouble you; but I remember you always and I keep a place for you in my heart, brimful of poetry.

Federico

---

[1] At the top of the letter he affixed a label for "Amatller Chocolates, Barcelona" depicting the story of Cinderella.

[2] Title of the 1931 play which bore the subtitle "Erotic Hallelujahs in Three Scenes."

TO HIS FAMILY

[Madrid, November, 1924]

Dear Everybody:

Did you receive my two cards? I'm very happy, extremely happy, because it's full steam ahead! My *Mariana Pineda* has succeeded in a way I did not expect and *The Shoemaker's Prodigious Wife* has excited enthusiasm because of its novelty. I'm putting the finishing touches on *Mariana Pineda*. As *impresario* [Gregorio] Martínez Sierra is enthusiastic, since he says that the work can be as successful as the *Tenorio* by Zorrilla.[1] Yesterday I ate at [Eduardo] Marquina's house and he told me *he'd cut off his right hand,* the one he writes with, if this work wasn't a hit in all the Spanish-speaking countries. [Enrique Díez-] Canedo, [Pedro] Salinas and Melchor [Fernández Almagro] heard it a few days ago and it left a deep impression on them. It seems that the Director (aggravated by the Manifesto of Blasco Ibáñez[2] and the Vera business) won't stage it, but we're going to rehearse it, in order to have it ready at the first opportunity, which will be within a year, according to what everybody believes. Of course, to stage it immediately is impossible and you'll understand why.[3] Even though they permitted it to be staged now, *it would cause a big row* in the theater and they would close it down, bringing about the ruin of the impresario, something that nobody wants. The circumstances are therefore impossible, but we're going ahead with sets, costumes, everything (!) and doing the rehearsals. I believe, and everybody believes the same, that it will be put on this year; and I've convinced myself that the success of the work does not have to, *nor must it* depend on politics, as Don Fernando [de los Ríos] might wish, since it's a *work of pure art,* a tragedy created by myself, as you know, without political interest and I'd like its success to be a *poetic* success—and it will be(!)— whenever it is performed.

And if it is not [a success], so be it: but it will always be a work of art. My friends feel the same way.

I must finish *The Shoemaker's Wife,* and do it well. It will be staged immediately, since [Catalina] Bárcena has one of the best parts. So, *both things will surely be staged.* Martínez Sierra shouts this from the rooftops and I, in addition, have sent Marquina to coax him a bit; and Marquina tells me that I have nothing to fear or doubt about him as impresario and that's enough.

I'm satisfied. I am progressively making my life and my name in the surest and purest manner. If I *catch on* in the theater, as I think I will, all the doors will gladly open up wide for me. The Atheneum of Barcelona invited me to give a lecture and a poetry reading, paying the trip, the expenses, and some money that they aren't sure about yet. The Atheneum of Murcia, also. Barcelona has called on [Antonio] Machado, Pérez de Ayala, and myself. And the automobile? How I long to get my hands on it! Within a few days I'll be with you. [Francisco A. de] Icaza is going to give a lecture. Paquito [García Lorca] ought to accompany him around. He's a little old man and one must treat him well. Paquito should meet him at the station and, even if it's a bit burdensome, he should forgive him, since he did very well by me. I love you all! Write me soon and forgive my delay. Hugs and kisses from your

Federico

[1] *Don Juan Tenorio* by José Zorrilla (1817–1893), the favorite of all the Spanish Don Juans.

[2] Vicente Blasco Ibáñez (1867–1928): prolific naturalist novelist. He was opposed to the military dictatorship (1923–1930) of General Miguel Primo de Rivera and a defender of republican ideals.

[3] The staging of the play was delayed because it might have been construed as a veiled attack on the dictatorship.

TO ANA MARIA DALI

[May, 1925]

Dear friend:

I don't know where I get the nerve to write you these lines. I've behaved like a scoundrel. Scoundrel. *Scoundrel.* SCOUNDREL. The scoundrels will go on climbing like this until one of them is as high as the luminous Citroen on top of the Eiffel Tower. But I know that you'll forgive me. I thought about writing to you every day; why didn't I do so? I don't know. I've thought about you all the more, but you probably think that I've forgotten you completely. On the seashore, beneath the olive trees, in the dining room of your house, on the Rambla de Figueras, and in the dining room of your house beneath the Divine Shepherdess, I possess a portfolio of memories of you and your laughter that is unforgettable. Besides, I never forget. I might not show any *signs of life,* but my intensity never varies (here a fly has placed the dot on the "i." Let us respect his aid and opinion).

How is your *aunt?* No matter how much I question your brother he never answers me on this point. And how is your father?

I think of Cadaqués. To me it is a landscape both eternal and present, but perfect. The horizon rises constructed like a great aqueduct. The silvery fish come forth to bathe in the moon and you will wet your braids in the water while the stuttering song of the motorboats comes and goes. When all of you stand in the doorway of your house, sunset will light up the coral that the Virgin holds in her hand. There's no one in the dining room. The maid has probably gone to the dance. The two black dancers of green and white crystal [the beaded curtains] will dance the sacred dance on the window and the door, which frightens the flies. Then my memory sits in an armchair. My memory dines on *crespell*[1] and red wine. You are laughing and your brother sounds like a big golden bee.[2] Beneath the white porticos one hears the sound of an accordion.

In Lydia's[3] doorway the Solid One[4] is calling, but no one answers. The two "brave fishermen of Culip" are crying with their voices perched on their knees. Lydia has died down. I should like to hear at this moment, Ana María, the noise of the chains of all the ships raising anchor in every sea . . . but the noise of the mosquito nets and the sea prevents me. Upstairs in your brother's room there's a saint on the wall. [Josep] Puig y Pujades,[5] with the little globe in his tummy, comes down the stairs. I'm too lonely in the dining room. But I can't get up. One of Salvador's drawings is tangled in my feet.[6] I wonder what time it is? . . . Right now I'd like to eat a piece of *Easter cake*. How does one say *"nublo"*?[7] *Nub*. . . . Through the window I see the dusty women in mourning passing by, crying bitterly on the way to see the notary.

So it is that I see myself in your dining room, *Señorita* Ana María. My memory is always intense. Remember how you laughed when you saw me with my gloves torn the day we were going to be shipwrecked?

I hope you'll find a way to forgive me. Don't be vindictive. All my sisters do is constantly ask me *what you are like*.

Regards to your father and *aunt*.

For you, my best regards.

Federico

Will you answer me?

---

[1] Traditional Catalonian fried sweet cakes.

[2] While drawing, Dalí sang, almost buzzing through closed lips (*The Unspeakable Confessions of Salvador Dalí,* New York, 1976, p. 42).

[3] Lydia Noguer: local character, fishwife, and keeper of a guest house.

[4] Title of a novel by Eugenio d'Ors (*La bien plantada*); Lydia believed she was the author's inspiration for the protagonist Teresa.

[5] Catalonian journalist.

[6] A reference to the string-like lines of Dalí's drawing.

[7] Ana María Dalí has noted that Lorca used a private, playful vocabulary with her. Lorca, she wrote, "liked to talk nonsense, invent words, give nicknames and crack jokes." He enjoyed learning Catalan and would constantly ask "How do you say . . . ?" until she answered him with the correct words (Antonina Rodrigo, *García Lorca en Cataluña,* Barcelona, 1975).

TO JOSE BELLO

[Summer, 1925]

[Fragment]

. . . Just as the light and weightless vegetation of saltpeter floats over the old walls of houses as soon as the owner gets careless, so the literary vocation springs up in you. That trip through Castile isn't original in its substance, but it is in its tone. (Faraway, among the chalk roses and canna lilies of Egypt, the city of Alexandria would lift its towers like stems of crystal and reddish salt.) Your fresh and ingenious prose recalls expressions from the correspondence of the great poet Lamartine addressed to his mother. It's too much to explain, but it's true.

Paquito [García Lorca] is going to Oxford in October and he'll surely see Filín. . . . He sends you hugs. . . . I imagine Paquito turned into an Englishman, very sober, very elegant, with that air of the wild duck that those strange insular people have. You and I are staying in Spain: he-goat, rooster, bull, dawns of fire and patios with white light, where the moisture brings forth touching blooms on the old heartless walls. If you could see how Andalusia really is! Just to walk one has to burrow corridors in the golden light like the moles in their dark element. The brilliant silks Michelangelize the behinds of opulent women. The roosters stick deluxe *banderillas* in the nape of dawn and I'm turning dark from the sun and the full moon. . . .

Federico

I read on your letter's postmark "Buitrago." Buitrago! I imagine a silver rock surrounded by vultures.[1] Down the highway go wineskin sellers, dealers, friars, people of the brown cape and saffron countenance. Deep in the background there's a garden. And that garden is your house, Mangirón. In the garden there are mallows, boxwood and lilies.

[1] *Buitre* means vulture.

[Granada, July, 1925]

Dear Melchorito:

Although you're no longer a friend and don't care for me at all, since I'm still very much a friend of yours and like you *sufficiently,* I'm permitting myself to write you to remind you that I exist.

I am in the country, and what heavenly country! Among all my memories I see your Moorish face, melancholy moon in the afternoon of the Regina [café].

I'm working . . . (don't say anything); I work in order to die living. I don't want to work to live dying.

I'm renewing myself. Thank God, in whom each passing day I place my desire and illusion.

I'm producing some strange dialogues, that are so superficial that they are very profound, and each one ends with a song. I've already done *"La doncella, el marinero y el estudiante"* ("The Maiden, the Sailor and the Student"), *"El loco y la loca"* ("The Madman and the Madwoman"), *"El teniente coronel de la Guardia Civil"* ("The Lieutenant Colonel of the Civil Guard"), *"Diálogo de la bicicleta de Filadelphia"* ("The Dialogue of the Philadelphia Bicycle"), and *"Diálogo de la danza"* ("Dialogue of the Dance"), which I'm working on now.

Pure poetry. Naked. I believe they hold great interest. They're more *universal* than the rest of my work (which, in parentheses, I don't find at all acceptable).

If you answer and if you love me, I'll send you some.

Write me immediately. Don't forget me. I wish you could come to Granada. I have a tremendous desire to give you a banquet with our friends. I'd toast you in verse.

Melchorito, tell me what's happening in Madrid.

Greet all our friends: Pepe Bergamín, and Guillén, and all the others.

Guillén is enchanting. I've spent some unforgettable moments in his house. If you see him tell him I'll write and send him a poem about my "Teresita."

Adiós. One embrace and another. Best regards to your family. The eighteenth is *my Saint's Day.* Write me before and after. *Adiós.*

Federico (ex-poet)

TO MELCHOR FERNANDEZ ALMAGRO

[Granada, the end of September, 1925]

Dear Melchorito:

You don't know how much we've grieved, I as well as my family, over the death of your poor Aunt Juana, so innocent and loving.

Just now I remember the day she made us hug each other in order for her to see the reality of our great friendship, blessed be her delicate and Christian soul a thousand times over!

And when are you visiting? We're all awaiting you with true affection and we're planning to dine together in your honor.

You don't have any idea of the enthusiasm your book aroused in Valdecasillas [Alfonso García Valdecasas] and [Antonio] Luna [García]. . . . And that's the way it ought to be, because the book is worthy of it![1]

I'm working a lot these days.

For the *first time in my life* I'm creating erotic poetry. A singular field has been opened to me, which is renewing me in an extraordinary way. I don't understand myself, Melchorito. My mother says: "You're still growing. . . ." And I, on the other hand, am *getting into problems* that I should have confronted long ago. . . . Am I backward? . . . What is this? It seems as though I've just attained my youth. That's why when I'll be sixty I won't be old . . . I'm never going to be *old*. *Adiós*. I feel like talking with you . . . and asking your advice.

Federico

---

[1] *Vida y obra de Angel Ganivet* by Melchor Fernández Almagro, Valencia, 1925.

TO ANA MARIA DALI

[Autumn, 1925]

My dear friend Ana María:

I've received your delightful letter in Granada. I've never forgotten you and if I haven't written you previously, it wasn't my fault but the fault of the somewhat foolish days I spent in Madrid. Now in Andalusia I'm another person. The same as I was in Cadaqués. How often have I recalled that shipwreck attempt of ours at Cap de Creus! And how delicious was that little rabbit which we ate with salt and *sand* at the foot of the orange eagle! That sea is my sea, Ana María!

It's very nice what you tell me about my poor little gloves (which were borrowed so as to make a good impression in your house), very nice.

All one's personality is embedded in gloves and hats after they've been *good and used*. Show me a glove and I'll tell you the character of its owner. . . . In the attics of the Pichot store there must be all sorts of gloves: black, kidskin, tiny white First Communion ones, lace gloves; it must be striking to see them in their wicker baskets . . . , especially the mother's, and the noise of the sea! I don't want to think about this theme of Ibsen. Let's think of *la Nini* who comes dressed as Orpheus singing like a drunken sailor on a tinplate seashell.

You say you've spent a wonderful summer which makes me very happy. A summer of canoes and classical poses. I, on the other hand, have had a pretty bad time. I've worked a lot, but I had a terrible desire to be near the sea. Later on I was and I cured myself completely. I can say that Málaga saved my life. In this way I was able to finish *Ifigenia*,[1] of which I'll send you a piece.

The business about Lydia is enchanting. I have her picture on my piano. Xenius[2] (Count of what?) says that *she* has the madness of Don Quixote (here one has to hold one's tongue and roll one's eyes), but he is wrong! Cervantes says of his hero "that his brain dried up," and that's true! The madness of Don Quixote is a dry madness, visionary, on a high plateau, an abstract madness, *without images*. . . . Lydia's madness is a watery madness,

64

gentle, full of seagulls and lobsters, a *malleable* madness. Don Quixote walks through the air and Lydia on the Mediterranean coast. That's the difference. And I want it to be clear so this superficiality of Xenius won't take root. How wonderful Cadaqués is! And how amusing to compare Lydia and the last of the knights errant! And you . . . do you forgive me this brief analysis of temperaments? I think so, because we've spoken of these things many times. And most of all . . . we were able to salvage our unique things, *the nets, the rocks, the highs and the lows.*

Didn't you know [Ernesto] Halffter? Isn't he a most interesting fool? He's *fool* enough to become a great artist. Why don't you and your brother come to Granada? My sisters will write inviting you. Regards to your aunt and father to whom I'm indebted for so many favors and affectionate treatment; regards to Salvador, and know that you're not forgotten by your friend.

Federico

A friend of all Catalonia, always! *Viva!*

What do you think of this portrait of that gent, your brother? Send me your answer. Don't forget this poor *shipwrecked* Andalusian.

---

[1] *El sacrificio de Ifigenia* was lost (José Luis Cano, *García Lorca: Biografía illustrada,* Barcelona, 1969, p. 57).

[2] Xenius, pen-name of Eugenio d'Ors (1883–1954), Catalonian writer and critic.

TO ANA MARIA DALI

[Early 1926]

My dear friend Ana María:

I haven't answered you before because for a number of days I've staged a magnificent attack of fever, and I had to give it the care it deserved.

It started with a very delicate trembling similar to a *tempo rubato* of Chopin, which I converted into a strong and serious rhythm with the intention of scaring the family and making them run upstairs and downstairs in great confusion. It worked out well.

Still I regret it wasn't an attack of *toothache,* which is the most sumptuous, best organized and most alarming attack, yet without after effects. This case was intense and left me yellow, with ears like paper. It's gone now.

Since the weather is nice, the young ladies of Granada go up to the whitewashed terraces to look at the mountains and not at the sea. The blondes go out into the sunshine and the brunettes stay in the shade. Those with chestnut hair are on the first floor looking at themselves in the mirror and putting on little celluloid combs.

In the afternoon they dress up in gauze and vaporous silks and go to the promenade where the diamond fountains flow and there are ancient tortures of roses and love's melancholy lingers on. Later on they fill up on cakes and chocolate *bon bons* in a store which ought to be called *Paris de Francia,* but is called *The Birdcage.* The social life of Granada is rich in poetry and lyric decadence.

The Mediterranean flora shines here with all the delicacy of its marvelous grays. Agave and olive trees. Yet the young ladies of Granada don't like the sea. They have big mother-of-pearl seashells with painted seascapes and that's the way they see it; they have big conch shells in their *living rooms* and that's the way they hear it.

Lucky you, Ana María, mermaid and shepherdess at the same time, olive dark and white with the cold foam. Little daughter of the olives and niece of the sea!

By now I'm slightly bored with Granada. I'd like to leave. Sometime, and perhaps soon, I'll have the pleasure of greeting you.

Until then here's the best of friendship from

Federico

Here come the beasts!

Did you notice how many beasts went to the tribute to Rusiñol?[1]

YES.

---

[1] Santiago Rusiñol: nineteenth-century landscape and portrait painter. Rusiñol founded a social group called "Noah's Ark" in which the members were named after animals.

TO JOSE MARIA CHACON Y CALVO

[Undated, latter half of 1920s]

[Drawing: a sailor]

This sad sailor smokes his pipe and reminisces.

If he is careless for a single moment, his eyes will fall forever to the bottom of the water. What a lethargic sea without sails and memories must be stirring at this very hour! What seas covered with dark roses and dead fish! And how real and true!

At the golden hour! Long live the hour! . . . We're all like the little sailor. From the harbors we hear the strains of accordions and the murky soapy noises of the docks, from the mountains we receive the dish of silence that the shepherds eat, but we don't hear more than our own distances. And what distances without end and without doors and without mountains!

I had to turn to you in this manner. Your sailor will understand my sailor.

Where are you: my dear José María?

Today I come out of my solitude to wave my white kerchief at you: North, South, East, West.

It's done! The little kerchief has a name.

In the country I *live*. I hope that you'll write me as always. Far from my friends in the heart of resplendent Andalusia, I feel lord of all this with my unknown court of brunette beauties. Goodbye sea: farewell José María. Count. Sir Count![1] A hug from

Federico (*Rex*)

Address:
Apeadero de San Pascual
Province of Granada

---

[1] José María Chacón y Calvo, Cuban writer and diplomatic attaché, really was a count, thus justifying Lorca's playful signature as "king."

[Granada, late February, 1926]

[Drawing: superimposed faces]

Dear Melchorito:

I, who imagined, I don't know why, that you were displeased with me, was overjoyed to see your letter from Zaragoza. I understand why the Aragonese city displeased you. Zaragoza is *falsified and turned into a comic operetta,* like the *jota* [Aragonese dance], and in order to find her ancient spirit you have to go to the Prado to admire the *exact portrait* done by Velásquez. There the Tower of San Pablo and the roofs of the Lonja are in their element against the pearly sky and the original silhouette of the houses. Today the city has departed. I, who have traveled throughout Aragón by train, believe that the old spirit of Zaragoza must be wandering around, riddled with white wounds, somewhere near Caspe, near the last gray rocks, where the hard wind flattens the shepherd and makes the light of the big stars shine *savagely.*

But Barcelona is very different, isn't it? There one finds the Mediterranean, the spirit, the adventure, the elevated dream of perfect love. There are palms, people from every country, surprising advertisements, gothic towers and a rich urban high tide created by typewriters. How I enjoy being there, with that air and *that passion!* It doesn't surprise me that they remember me, because I got along with them all and my poetry was given a better reception than it really deserved. [José María de] Sagarra showed me such deference and friendship that I'll never forget it. Besides, I, who am a *ferocious Catalanist,* identified greatly with those people, so fed up with Castile and *so creative.*

I've kept up to date with that region through my friend and inseparable companion Salvador Dalí, with whom I carry on an abundant correspondence. He has invited me to spend another season at his house, which I'll certainly do, since I have *to pose* for him.

I have many secret projects that I'll tell you about. I want to publish. Because if I don't do it now, I'll never do it, and that's bad. But I want to do it right. I've worked on the arrangement of my books. They are three. *The choicest.* The things in them are things that should be there. The book I've done of brief songs is interesting. Since you don't remember them, you think that they've *been revised already.* Nothing further from the truth. *They've been left unscathed.* Poor little things! But they have *something,* and that something is that which can't be imitated. I am not *carried away by music,* like certain *young poets.* I grant *love* to the word (!) and not to the sound. My songs are not made of ash. How useful it has been to have put them away. Bless me! Now in this revision I've given them the final touch, and it's done! I dedicate one part of this book to Jorge Guillén's daughter Terestita in this way: "To Teresita Guillén, playing her six-note piano." All of them are dedicated to children. The other books are dedicated to adults. To you, to [Pedro] Salinas, etc. I've worked hard. I want to go to Madrid soon . . . , but I'll go to Figueras and then to Toulouse with Paquito [García Lorca]. The *literary atmosphere* of Madrid seems to me too *stingy and mean.* Everything turns into gossip, cabals, calumnies and American banditry. I feel like refreshing my poetry and my heart in foreign waters, in order to produce greater riches and expand my horizons. I'm sure that a new period is beginning now for me.

I want to be a poet, from head to toe, living and dying by poetry. I'm beginning to *see clearly.* A high awareness of my future work is taking hold of me and an almost dramatic feeling of my responsibility constrains me . . . I don't know . . . it seems that *I'm giving birth* to new forms and an absolutely defined balance.

Paquito is still in Bordeaux. Soon he'll go to Toulouse and then to London. I'm leaving immediately. I feel like giving you and Guillén a hug, you are both so good to me. I was born for my friends, but *I was not born* for mere *acquaintances.*

[Drawing of Pierrot]

TO MELCHOR FERNANDEZ ALMAGRO

[Granada, February or March, 1926]

Dear Melchorito:

I received your letter. I've got one foot in the stirrup. The matter of my books has been completely resolved. I'll tell you how I'm going to do them. I want the three to come out in the month of April. Right now, I'd like to resolve *Mariana Pineda,* since [Gregorio] Martínez Sierra has behaved like a. . . . But Martínez Sierra *ignores my fantasy.* He doesn't know what *trouble he's taken on with me.*

I think it's an excellent idea to put on my puppet shows in the new puppet stage. In a few days I'll be there and I'll deliver them. It seems to me that they can be very amusing. I fixed them up a bit. The songs now seem delightful . . . but who will play the part of Don Cristóbal? On Tuesday, at the latest, I'll be there. Do you want me to notify you? Answer me by return mail.

What is turning out to be a big nuisance is *Mariana Pineda.* We'll see about it . . . but will someone want *to produce it*? I would like that for my family's sake.

There's no doubt that I really have *a feeling for the theater.* These past few days it has occurred to me to do a comedy whose chief characters are *photographic enlargements.* Those people we see in doorways. Newlyweds, sergeants, dead girls, an anonymous crowd full of mustaches and wrinkles. It should be terrible. If *I focus it* well, it will possess pathos without consolation. In the midst of those people I will place an authentic fairy.

Could we put it on in Cipriano's puppet theater? I'm hoping to finish it soon. *Adiós.* Answer me. A hug for Cipriano [Rivas Cherif] and another strong one for you from

Federico

We were in Calahorra. I am sending you a splendid photo of the castle.
Regards to everybody.

[Mr. Jorge Guillén (Professor of Spanish Language and Literature). Reina Victoria Hotel, Murcia.]

[Granada, March 2, 1926]

Answer me immediately
My foot is in the stirrup to
go to Madrid.

My dear Jorge:

I dedicate every day to your penetrating and delicate friendship. I'm satisfied to have you, and a few others (very few), as friends. The memory of you and your wife and children is a *fiesta* of smiles and affection. It's impossible to forget little Teresa.

What moves me most about your friendship is the interest that you take in the poet. If I publish, it's so that you (my three!) may have the books. *At heart* I don't find my work illuminated with the light that I'd like . . . I have too much chiaroscuro. You're too generous with me. Gen-er-ous.

*

The people found my lecture on Góngora[1] very entertaining because I proposed to *explain The Solitudes*[2] so that they should understand them and should not be blockheads . . . and they understood! At least that's what they said. I worked on it for three months. I'll make you a copy and send it on. You tell me *as a teacher* what critical blunders it contains.

But it was *serious*. My voice was another's. It was a serene voice and full of *years* . . . , as old as I am! It hurt me a little to see that I am capable of giving a lecture without poking fun at the audience. I'm becoming serious. I spend a lot of time in pure sadness. At times I surprise myself when I see that I am *intelligent*. Old age!

I'm doing a lot of work now. I'm finishing the *Gypsy Ballads*. New themes and old suggestions. The Civil Guard comes and goes through all Andalusia. I would like to read you the erotic ballad of the "Unfaithful Wife" or "Preciosa and the Wind." "Preciosa and the Wind" is a gypsy ballad which is a *myth* invented by me. In this part of the book I try to harmonize the *mythological gypsy* with the purely ordinary one of the present day, and the result is strange, but I believe it has a new beauty. I want the pictures I draw of the characters to be *understood* by themselves, to be visions of the world in which they live, and in this way make the ballad snug and solid as a rock. I've spent a *month and a half* composing the ballad of the "Beaten Gypsy," but . . . I'm satisfied. The ballad is set. The blood which comes out of the gypsy's mouth is no longer blood . . . it is air!

It will be a book of ballads and one could say that it is a book of Andalusia. That at least! Andalusia doesn't turn her back on me . . . ; I know that she hasn't gone to bed with an Englishman . . . , but I don't want to go on talking of this. Don't you know why?[3]

*

Now that you're in Murcia, I'm reminded of its tower and of [Juan] Guerrero [Ruiz], such an amiable and charming friend with whom I behave so badly. Give him a hug in my name.

*

These days I'm working on a *long poem*. The "Didactic Ode to Salvador Dalí" already has one hundred and fifty alexandrines, but this poem will surely have four hundred. It's called "The Siren and the Soldier." It tells how a carabineer kills a little mermaid with one rifle shot. It's a tragic idyll. At the end there will be a great lament of mermaids, a lament rising and falling at the same time, like seawater, while the carabineers place the mermaid in the flag room. All this done with great lyric effect. The same lyricism for the carabineer as for the mermaid. A flat light and *love* and *serenity* in the form. It will be a *big bore,* but the story moves me profoundly. It's the myth of the useless beauty of the sea. Later I would like the water to be still, so that I can minutely describe a wave (the first one) and then the second and then the third, and so on until we run into a little boat . . . a little boat where the poet will dream his last dream. This ending of shifting water could be admirable if I *achieve* it. Don't say anything to anybody about this. I want to do it without being asked about it. Tell me what you think. Shall I put my maximum effort into this? Can I rise to the challenge? The Lord only knows.

73

This is how the poem begins:

> The scalene landscape of foam and olives
> cuts its profiles in the hard sky
> Deep light without a fold of mist draws taut
> like the rosy shoulder of a naked swimmer.
>
> Boats and roosters spread their wings of feathers and linen.
> Dolphins in a line play at broken bridges.
> The afternoon's moon rises round
> and the chaste hill exudes whispers and sweet scents.
>
> At the water's edge the sailors sing
> songs of bamboo and refrains of snow.
> Equivocal maps shine in their eyes.
> Ecuador without light and China without air.
>
> Cornets of copper blare beneath the arches
> where in the morning the fisherman swears.
> Cornets of copper played by carabineers
> in the battle with the sea and its folk.

And then, after some more stanzas, I say:

> The night disguised in a mule skin
> pushes the lateen sailed boats along.
> The graceful waistline is full of shadow
> and the sea loses shame and golden virtues.
>
> Oh muses dancing on tender wet feet
> in pretty trinities on the succulent turf!
> Accept my offerings giving the rarified air
> nine different songs and only one word.

And then the narrative begins. Doing this poem is very entertaining. If you answer immediately, I'll send you a gypsy ballad. And you? Why don't you send me some of your things? I'd like to do an article on your verses in a first rate magazine coming out in Granada by the up-and-coming kids with talent. Granada is stupendous! I direct the magazine *from afar*. I've added a subtitle: "Review of happiness and literary play." Here we will publish the portrait, presiding over the magazine, of the marvelous professor of poetry who constructs his poems in Murcia, beneath the perfect lamp of Minerva.

Adiós, dearest Jorge. I send you my affectionate admiration along with that of my friends in Granada, who *exchange* your beautiful and exact *décimas*,[4] which betray your exquisite hand, lightly poised over the white page.

Adiós, a very strong embrace.

Federico

> Words of crystal and dark breeze
> truly round ones, the mute fish speak.
> Academy, in the cloister of the rainbows
> beneath the dense and penetrable ecstasy.
> . . . .

This is from a "Solitude" that I am composing in honor of Góngora. You'll enjoy it when it's finished.

You can't say that I'm wasting time!

I'm hacking away . . . a hardworking guy.

Answer me before I leave for Madrid.

---

[1] Luis de Góngora (1561–1627): last of the great poets of the Spanish Golden Age, known for his ornate style. He was also the subject of outlandish celebrations held in his honor by members of Lorca's generation, but in this letter Lorca assures Guillén his approach was *serious*. The lecture Lorca referred to is included in *Deep Song and Other Prose*, edited and translated by Christopher Maurer, New York, 1980.

[2] *The Solitudes* (*Las Soledades*): an unfinished pastoral idyll considered to be Góngora's masterpiece.

[3] Guillén has said he didn't.

[4] Stanzas of ten octosyllabic lines.

TO MELCHOR FERNANDEZ ALMAGRO

[Granada, February or March, 1926]

Dear Melchorito:

The *up-and-coming* young men of Granada are going to produce a magazine. They call it *Granada,* because they can't help it, because it's being done for free by some typographers. It's called *Granada,* but, on the other hand, it's subtitled "Review of happiness and literary play," and that tells the whole story. I'm thinking of contributing to every issue, since *it can be* a very delightful item. It will contain things by Dalí. And they'll publish reproductions of Manuel Angeles [Ortiz]. And hilarious photos of poets and friends. I hope that you'll promptly send a beautiful article. You have no idea how these fellows *like you.* In the first issue it'll be me, you and Manuel-Angeles. Will you do it? I hope so, since it would be *terrible* if you didn't do so immediately. [Jorge] Guillén will be submitting things and I think everybody will follow suit, since these fellows are thinking of publishing only brief *notes* and things they judge acceptable. I hope you won't disregard my request. In a few days you'll be receiving news of my arrival. You should ask for some things from our friends who might want to help with such a lovely and natural project.

A very strong hug from

Federico

Mail care of Antonio A. de Cienfuegos. Plaza de Santa Ana, 18. Thanks, Melchor!

TO ANA MARIA DALI

[Early 1926]

[Miss Ana María Dalí
(Monturiol, 24)
Figueras.
Province of Gerona.]

Dear Ana María:

I've been hearing rumors that your brother has gone to France and some other *news items* that I didn't believe, naturally. Since he had agreed to send me some drawings for my books and hasn't, I thought it possible that he could have made a little excursion to the neighboring country. Tell me the facts about all this and dispel these rumors.

At home we've been upset since we've been out of touch with my brother in Paris for more than two months. I'm doing a lot of work now. In my first book I dedicated a song to you. I don't know if it's to your taste, but I've tried to pick one of the nicest. Answer, and if your brother is there, tell him not to be such a loafer, and that I want his drawings.

Regards to your parents and friends. *Adiós,* Ana María. The most affectionate friendship from your friend and *little fool.*

Federico

Acera del Casino, 31. Granada.

TO JORGE GUILLEN

[Granada, July 1926]

[Mr. Jorge Guillén (poet), Atheneum, Valladolid.]

My dear Jorge:

I seek your kind consideration. My affection for you makes it seem impossible that we shouldn't share the enchanting bond of correspondence.

It just can't be. I want to write to you and to hear from you frequently.

I'm in the country. Andalusia is on fire. I drink spring water and eat apples (I think of your children), apples bitter and sweet. What I haven't been able to find until now is "the pure dove coffee" which the *budding seraph* Gerardo Diego drinks in his cell. How much more beautiful and unique it is to drink Puerto Rican coffee! And how much more strange! The pure dove coffee seems to be a product obtained as a wartime necessity. It has a frightening *reality*. Here I stop. Why continue?

I hope that neither you nor your wife will forget me. And that you'll write. I'll send you new poems and you will do the same for me.

Affectionate regards to Germaine and the children. A cordial embrace from your friend, admirer and *pole* [opposite].

Federico

I'm sending this letter to the "Atheneum" because I don't remember your address. My address is:

Apeadero de San Pascual
Prov. de Granada.

If you write me immediately send the letter to this address and, if not, to the Acera del Casino, 31, but write soon.

Have you seen [Jean] Cassou's commentary in *Mercure* on the ode?

Adiós.

Wash your eyes with the soap of language.

(Only in the morning.)

YOU AND I ARE POETS!
POETS!
TO OUR JOY
(VERY OLD POETS)
1926

TO JORGE GUILLEN

[Postcard. Lanjarón (Granada).]

[Lanjarón, August 6, 1926]

[Mr. Jorge Guillén (poet), Atheneum, Valladolid.]

Many thanks for the card.

But I'm ambitious and expect a letter. I'm in the Sierra Nevada and I often go down to the sea in the afternoon. What an amazing sea is the Mediterranean of the South! South, South! (wonderful word, south). The most incredible fantasy develops in a logical and serene manner. The Andalusian features are intermixed with traits of a fixed and filtered north.

I'm working as usual. I've *resolved* to finish the *Gypsy Ballads*. Here I've produced two more ballads that have taxed my efforts extraordinarily. Also, I want to send you an epistle on poetry and poetic art which will be a lengthy poem, *monotonous*, structured, anti-decorative and *boring*. Ay, Poetry of my heart! Ay, Rhetoric of my voice!

Lots of love to Germaine and the children, Teresita and Claudio. An embrace for you from

Federico

TO EDUARDO MARQUINA[1]

[August, 1926]

Dear Marquina:

Margarita Xirgu agreed to respond with her impression of the exceedingly troublesome *Mariana Pineda*. She hasn't done so. I know her mother died, but that was some time ago, and besides on account of that she's not going to retire from the stage. I don't know what to do, and I am also annoyed because, since my parents don't see *anything practical* in my literary endeavors, they are displeased with me and do nothing but point to the example of my brother Paquito, a student at Oxford loaded with laurels. Although it might be troublesome for you, I beg you not to forget me in this inconclusive situation. The summer is coming to an end and I am still left hanging, without the least prospect of getting on with my work as a dramatic poet, in which I have so much faith and so much joy. Don't forget to write and tell me your opinion and what you think. Should I write to Margarita? If you consider the subject a lost cause, let me know that as well. Greetings to everyone in your family. Eduardo, surely you will excuse these irksome problems I cause you. Don't forget me! Here's a big hug from

Federico

Acera del Casino, 91, Granada

[1] Eduardo Marquina: poet and friend of the Dalí family. He and Lorca had known each other since meeting in Madrid in 1919.

[Granada, September 2, 1926]

[Mr. Jorge Guillén (poet), Atheneum, Valladolid.]

My dear Jorge:

In spite of your promise I have not yet received a letter and know nothing of your doings this summer. I *have decided* to take the exams for a professorial post in Literature, because I think I have the vocation (it is slowly growing in me) and the capacity for enthusiasm.

Besides, I want to be independent and to affirm my personality within my family, who give me, naturally, everything I need and require. The minute I mentioned it in the house, it made my parents extremely happy and they've promised me, if I begin to study promptly, to give me money for a trip to Italy, which I've dreamed about for years.

I am *decided* and want to be even more decided, but *I don't know how things are done.* Of course, I'll have to bang my head against the wall in order to accomplish this, because I don't eat or drink or understand anything but Poetry. And that's why I turn to you. What do you think I ought to do in order to begin in earnest my preparation for a professorship . . . yes! Professor of poetry? What must I do? Where do I go? What should I study? What *disciplines* would be suitable for me? Answer me. I'm in no rush, but I want to do this in order to justify my poetic (now definitive) attitude.

Be good and answer me immediately. I'll be your pupil and Salinas' and take a vow of obedience and academic fervor.

On the other hand, I don't have another choice and I feel my voice poor, but illuminated in other people's reception rooms . . . and besides . . . is this badly thought out? Can I really do it?

Adiós. Don't forget me.

Right now I'm in the "Huerta de San Vicente," in the plain of Granada. There is so much jasmine in the garden and so many "ladies of the night" that in the morning they give everybody in the house a lyrical headache, as marvelous as that which one suffers from water retention.

And yet, nothing is excessive! That's the amazing thing about Andalusia.

If you answer, I'll send poems. Send me some of yours.

Regards to your wife and children (charming children).

Awaiting your advice I send you a hug

Federico

Send me Salinas' address.

Send your letter to the Acera del Casino, 31. Granada.

My God! Don't go taking my letter as a lyric joke because it is expressed *off the cuff* and without a preamble.

Let me stay a little longer in the playground, since I will have plenty of time to put on gray flannel and the cold airs of meditation.

TO JORGE GUILLEN

[Granada, September 9, 1926]

[Mr. Jorge Guillén (poet), Atheneum, Valladolid.]

Dear Jorge:

You don't know how grateful I am for your advice. The notes that I'll take will be noteworthy because I always focus on the strange things about an author. But besides this *fixed schedule* of readings, do you think I should work with someone? Go somewhere else? Should I go as a "reader"? Because to wait and *read* in Granada until the competition seems too much. Don't you think so? Tell me something about this. Also, will it take much time? This is important, because I have *to have a position*. Imagine if I should like to get married. Would I be able to do it? No. And this is what I want to resolve. I am beginning to see that my heart seeks a garden and a little fountain as in my first poems. Not a garden of divine flowers and opulent butterflies, but a garden of air and monotonous leaves where my five senses, domesticated, may look at the sky.

Tell me what I can be a professor of or . . . something! Don't get the idea that I am *involved* with a particular girl, but isn't this imminent? My heart seeks a garden, etc., etc. . . . (What etceteras loaded down with poetry and novelty!)

*

I've already told you in a postcard that your poems pleased me very much. They are pure and profound. An invitation to astronomy. The miniaturized sea and the jelly sailors in so much recent poetry drown in the monotonous and refined "hard green water" that flows like a marble frieze to the eternal and congenial site of true poetry which is love, effort and renunciation. (Saint Sebastian.) When poetry is filled with trumpets and garlands it turns the academy into a counting house. I can only tell you that I hate the organ, the lyre and the flute. I love the human voice. The solitary human voice impoverished by love and removed from landscapes *that kill*. The voice must detach itself from the harmonies of things and from *the concert of nature* in order that its single note may flow. Poetry is another world. The doors by

84

which it escapes must be closed to vulgar ears and loose tongues. One must lock oneself in with it. And there let the divine and poor voice sound while we cap the fountain. No to the fountain.

When I say voice I mean the poem. The poem which is not dressed isn't a poem, as unworked marble isn't a statue.

*

That is why I like your poetry so much. That is what I think poetry should be. And nevertheless, I believe we all sin. The poem that pierces the heart like a sword has yet to be written. I'm amazed when I consider that the emotion of composers (Bach) is based on and is surrounded by a perfect mathematics. Your poems possess (especially the *décimas*) poles and an equator. Just so! Exalted poet.

Now let us say: God free us from the tropics![1] (Pray for me.)

*

Because I am a sinner. I've often destroyed divine moments of poetry so as not to suffer the fever on my hands. Now I am another and I'll be more so in the future.

*

You can't imagine how I've laughed with that delightful sickness, "the pain of the white shoe." Exquisite. It's a marvelous pain that should strike Juan Ramón (Jiménez) in that fantastic eye of his.

Write and tell me things about the professorship. Give me encouragement, or suggest something else. And now after kissing the children and giving regards to Germaine for me, listen to this new gypsy ballad.

[Two poems were enclosed: *"Reyerta de mozos"* ("Brawl"), and *"San Miguel Arcángel,"* later published with variations in *Romancero gitano.*]

That's it. Don't forget to write. I'm working hard. I'm going to give three lectures. "The Myth of Saint Sebastian." I should like it if you could send me a photo of the "Saint Sebastian" of Berruguete. In the second lecture I'll show slides of several famous ones. If you can't do this, ask [Gómez] Orbaneja, who will do it, because he knows how I value his friendship. WE WANT TO BRING YOU HERE. I'll speak to you about it later. *Adiós.* Regards to everybody, and a strong embrace from

Federico
(incorrigible poet)

I would also like *to go as a lecturer* for a season. Paris would be ideal. Would I be able to do this? What's happening is this. My family will give me all the money I want and more, as soon as they see me on the way . . . how shall I put it . . . officially. That's it, officially!

But for the first time they *oppose* my writing poetry without thinking of anything else. A little show of effort on my part is enough for them to be satisfied. That's why I'd like to start to do something . . . official. Being a lecturer would be good before any examination and useful as preparation for a professorship. You've been one yourself, right?

Fill me in.

I've already sent for the card file. What fantastic notes will fill it! By the way, I feel a tremendous itch and a keen desire to get away from Spain. *Once outside* I'd be able to do my "Diego Corrientes"[2] and other intense poems that I can't look at here. Besides I'll be free (in the good sense of the word) of the family and I'll go off alone to the mountains to see the dawn with no need to be home on time. Dawn of responsibility. I'll be responsible for the sun and the breezes. Threshold of paternity.

Answer me and tell me what steps I've got to take to become a lecturer. [Pedro] Salinas will tell me how to go about becoming a professor.

But what if I don't have the aptitude? Because I'm not intelligent or hard working (a good for nothing!). Then . . . we'll see!

A hug from

Federico

Don't forget to answer me, because time is passing.
[The following poem appears on the reverse of the letter.]

SONG

Slow perfume and heart without spectrum,
air definitive in its roundness,
fixed heart, conqueror of the North,
I'd like to leave you and be alone.

In the decapitated north star.

In the broken and submerged compass.

[1] Not even Jorge Guillén, the recipient of the letter, knows exactly what Lorca meant by "tropics" except that the word plays off the statement that Guillén's poems have "poles" and an "equator."

[2] No such poem has been found.

TO MELCHOR FERNANDEZ ALMAGRO

[Granada, October 20-28, 1926]

I don't know who these respectable gentlemen are.[1] But there's no doubt that they're charming. They've given me an idea of what Spain was like in the darkness of the nineteenth century. They seem to be musicians. Aren't they musicians? You who are an extraordinary connoisseur of the last century should be able to identify them immediately.

That's why I'm sending you these delicate little stamps, born on a night of Italian opera, night of warm vocals and snow on the roof tops. Of the four, Cuyás interests me most (who is Cuyás?), because he dies young and he's like a Bécquer in wintry dress, half Roman, half professor of literature. The woman who's looking through her glasses doesn't wear white crinoline as some heedless poets might suppose. You only have to look at the color of her brow to know that this lady of illusions is dressed in the color of bone and carries a skull crowned with roses in her hands. The others eat homemade bread watered with the characteristic tears of the epoch.

Dear Melchorito:

It's been some time since I've been able to write you a letter *with pleasure*. Today I write you this one very slowly and with real affection.

We've celebrated the homage to Soto[2] which was very successful. Tomorrow we'll unveil the ceramic plaque which we dedicated to him and we'll read a beautiful poem sent by Gerardo [Diego] for this occasion. You should write, in spite of everything, an article on Soto and the Atheneum for the *Defensor*. We'd like you to propose whatever occurs to you that can be done right away, and of course you must come to give a lecture and spend a few days with me. Emilio Prados has been here (he left yesterday). He took all my books and they *will come out* as soon as possible.

I dedicate one to you together with [Pedro] Salinas and [Jorge] Guillén, my best friends.[3] The three most delightful people I have ever known. Tell me what you think. Should the three come out at the same time or separately? Answer me.

We've had a marvelous time. We've taken automobile trips to the *sierra*, to Alfaguara, to Guadix and the castle of Calahorra, to Jaén and to beautiful Antequera. I wish you'd come and follow the same route.

Emilio is also going to do a beautiful edition of the "Ode" with drawings and statues to give as a gift to friends. Emilio has given me a collection of books of popular songs and ballads which I plan to organize right away. With these, at last, will come to light the Granadan *cancionero*,[4] so important for this type of still unpublished study. As you see I have an enormous amount of work. Right now *work is underway* on the Ode to Juan Belmonte which can be a stupendous thing if it comes out the way I see it.

Wave
Wave
Wave
Wave to me, Melchorito!

Three minutes of rest.

Now we turn to an ugly subject, hateful but one which I have to resolve. You want to help me? Yes? Then listen.

As you know, I delivered the hateful *Mariana Pineda* to Xirgu for her to read. This lady promised to answer me. But she hasn't done so. Her mother died. I sent her a telegram of condolence. She hasn't answered. I wrote to [Eduardo] Marquina (the fresh Marquina). He didn't answer me. I wrote him again. Still no answer. What should I do? My family, displeased with me because they say I'm not doing anything, don't let me leave Granada. I'm sad as you must suppose. Granada is odious if you have to live here. Here, in spite of everything, I'm *drowning*.

I have various projects, but I want to finish this disastrous venture of mine in the theater's den, a venture which I undertook to please my parents and I have failed with the whole business. I'm not sorry for myself. But I am for my father who's so kind and would have been overjoyed with the debut of this work. You're going to do me a little favor. You're going to visit Eduardo Marquina on my behalf, in view of the fact that he doesn't answer me and you're going to tell him to do me the favor of asking Xirgu her opinion of the play and what she's going to do about it and if she's not going to do anything that she return the copy she's holding. Marquina would be delighted not to see me. He would be satisfied if *Mariana Pineda* is not produced and I've bothered him enough already. Well then, I don't know, dear Melchorito, if I should be grateful to him or not, because his attitude (which was reflected in the interview with Milla in the *Esfera*) is equivocal and nebulous. Go, at once, to Marquina and tell him that you're coming from me (and you're interested yourself, naturally, since it concerns me) in order to ask him about the business with *Mariana*. He'll probably give you a *song and dance*. Don't pay attention. Just insist and tell him to speak to Xirgu and that she should state her opinion clearly. Don't put off doing this favor for me. If Xirgu doesn't want to put on my work and returns the original, you keep it as a gift of my failed attempt in an age in which *there is no theater* and we must resign ourselves. But word it so that Marquina has to give his reasons. Don't delay. I want to know what's happening. It's a real shame I lost all that time! But there's *bad faith* in everybody. Marquina puts on a mask of wanting to *protect me,* but I don't believe him. Rotten people and cretinism everywhere.

Forgive me. There's nobody better than you for this. You're Marquina's friend and he speaks well of you and *is indebted* to you for your benevolent reviews.

You can do this better than I. Be strong and firm. Whatever you do will be well done. I'll accept whatever you do. Take the disposition and attitude which seem appropriate. And if you don't want to do this, for whatever reasons, I won't be displeased. Just tell me. If you decide and wish to, do it immediately and describe the course *of events* to me. Of course, if *Mariana is presented,* I would gain everything with my family.

It's done.

Granada is admirable. Autumn begins with all the elegance and light given off by the *sierra.* The first snows have fallen. The yellows begin, infinite and deep, to play with twenty shades of blue. It's an amazing richness, a richness which is stylized and wholly unattainable. Granada, definitely, is not pictorial, not even for an impressionist. It's not pictorial, just as a river is not architectonic. Everything runs, plays and escapes. Poetic and musical. A city of grays without a skeleton. A vertebrate melancholy.

That's why I can stay here. Good-bye, Melchorito. Regards to our friends. A very strong hug for you from

Federico

Don't forget this!
Answer at once!

[1] Four stamps were affixed to the letter picturing the following Spanish personages: Saldoni y Remendo, Santiago de Masarnau, Aspá and Cuyás.
[2] Pedro Soto de Rojas: seventeenth-century Granadan poet, follower of Góngora.
[3] The book *Canciones* (1921–1924) published in Málaga in 1927 is dedicated "To Pedro Salinas, Jorge Guillén, and Melchorito Fernández Almagro."
[4] *Cancionero:* a collection of historical songs and ballads.

[Granada, November, 1926]

Dear Melchorito:

Thank you very much for intervening in the matter of *Mariana Pineda*. Let's see if we can end it once and for all. You haven't given me your opinion on whether the three books should come out at the same time or separately. Let me know.

I await the results of your efforts but without any hopes.

Marquina is adopting equivocal attitudes and if *Mariana* is put on he'll say it "was done by him." The theater is disgusting.

Now I'm beginning to work. I'm finishing the *Gypsy Ballads* and I'm *being teased* by a long poem, still unshaped, but lyrical, with a sharp and fabulous lyricism, suggestive and many sided. I don't know. But it will come out! You know that I've been stroking the idea of this poem for many years.

Granada in the rain has the divine light of a pensive brow which reminds us of childhood. The light of 6:30 in the afternoon, when we turn the corner upon leaving school.

Adiós. Won't you come? Valle-Inclán[1] will almost certainly come, because the Atheneum will bring him. The steps are being taken. Greetings to your friends.

An affectionate embrace from

Federico

---

[1] Ramón María del Valle-Inclán (1866–1936): major novelist of the "Generation of 1898."

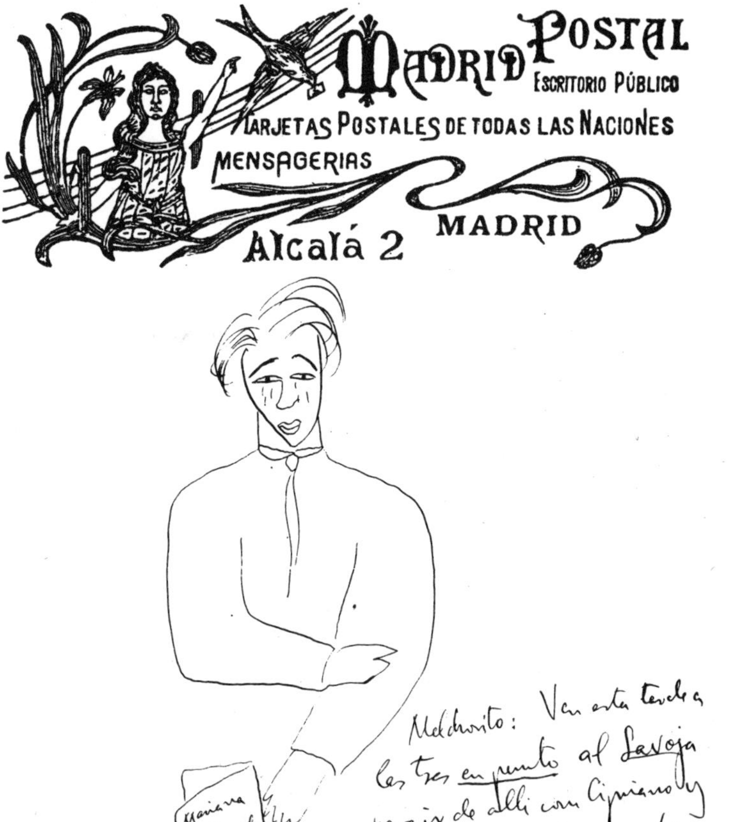

Postcard to Melchor Fernández Almagro, *c.* autumn, 1926.

¡Queridísimo Don Manuel!.
¿Se hace por fin el azulejo a Glinka?
¡Mucho me gustaría tener noticias afirmativas de
este asunto tan agradable y tan justo! yo por mi
parte estoy dispuesto a tender un puente de oro para
que se realice! (contésteme sí o no como Cristo nos
enseña)

No se puede usted imaginar como le recuerdo cuando
toco la guitarra y quiero sacar ¡a la fuerza! su maravilloso
Homenaje a Debussy, del que no consigo mas que

Opening of a letter to Manuel de Falla, August, 1923 (see p. 43).

In the underground baths of the Alhambra. Left to right: Adolfo Salazar, Manuel de Falla, Angel Barrios, Federico García Lorca. Seated: Francisco García Lorca.

Federico García Lorca with Salvador Dalí in Cadaqués, *c.* 1927.

Federico García Lorca with Angel del Río and a neighbor's children, in Vermont, 1929.

Federico García Lorca with Catalan friends in Barcelona, 1927; the
names are in Lorca's handwriting. Left to right: Manuel Font, J.V. Foix,
Sebastián Gasch, Luis Montanyà, Josep Carbonell, Lorca, Salvador Dalí,
M. A. Cassanyes.

Standing, left to right: Vicente Aleixandre, Federico García Lorca,
Pedro Salinas, Rafael Alberti, Pablo Neruda, Jose Bergamin, Manolo
Altolaguirre, the wife of Rafael Alberti. Seated, front-left: Miguel
Hernández; in center: Luis Cernuda; partly hidden: Santiago Ontañón.

Federico García Lorca with his mother, 1935.

Federico García Lorca in front of a poster for La Barraca, his traveling theater troupe, 1934.

TO JORGE GUILLEN

[Granada, November 8, 1926]

[Jorge Guillén (Professor of Literature), Murcia University]

> Guillén! Guillén! Guillén!
> Why hast thou abandoned me?

It's no good. I always wait for your letter, but it never comes. Do you realize my books are already at the printer? Please answer this question by return mail: should the three come out at the same time? Or at intervals?

I dedicate one to Pedro Salinas, Melchorito [Fernández Almagro] and YOU.

I'm no more gallant than your lordship. And what about those poems?

In spite of everything I want to be sure to read you this fragment of the "Ballad of the Civil Guard," which I'm composing at present.

I began it two years ago, remember?

[The poem included in this letter appears with slight variations in *Romancero gitano* with the title *"Romance de la Guardia Civil Española"* ("Ballad of the Spanish Civil Guard").]

I've done up to here. Now the Civil Guard comes and destroys the city. Later the guards go to their barracks and there they drink toasts with Cazalla anisette to the death of the gypsies. The scenes of pillage will be grand. At times, without one knowing why, they will turn into Roman centurions. This ballad will be very long, but one of the best. The final apotheosis of the Civil Guard is exciting.

Once this ballad and the "Ballad of the Martyrdom of the Gypsy Saint Olalla of Mérida" is ended the book will be completed. It'll be terrific. I think it's a good book. Afterwards I'll never touch this theme again, *never! never!*

Good-bye . . .

> Guillén, Guillén, Guillén,
> Why hast thou abandoned me?

Federico

TO JORGE GUILLEN

[Granada, January, 1927]

1.9.2.7.

[*Drawing*]
[1st page]

HALLELUJAH   Teresita
                               Claudio

Dear Jorge:

[2nd page]
[a drawing]

Love
in
1927

                                         Jorge

[3rd page]

A big hug for you and yours in 1927. There are lots of things
I have to tell you. I'm ready to subscribe to *Verso y Prosa*. Delighted. I've already gotten several subscriptions. But I can't send
you anything yet. Later on. And of course they won't be gypsy
ballads. This gypsy *myth of mine* annoys me a little. They con-
fuse my life and character. This isn't what I want at all. The
gypsies are a theme. And nothing more. I could just as well be
a poet of sewing needles and hydraulic landscapes. Besides, this
gypsyism gives me the appearance of an uncultured, ignorant
and *primitive poet* that you know very well I'm not. I don't want
to be typecast. I feel as if they're chaining me down. NO (as
[Eugenio d'] Ors would say).

You've probably received *Litoral*. Lovely, right? But did you
notice how horribly my Ballads came out?

They contained more than ten(!) enormous errata and were
completely ruined. Most of all the ballad of Antoñito el Camborio. What great anguish it caused me, dear Jorge, to see them
broken, undone, without that *strength* and flintlike *grace* that
for me they seem to possess! Emilio [Prados] agreed to send me
proofs but he never did. The morning when I received the magazine I cried, I literally *cried,* it was such a shame. I sent a tele-

gram to Prados and he became irked and put the blame on my impossible manuscript, etc., etc. But since he knows me he should have known better. Just today I received all my originals with a *laconic* letter asking me to *correct* them and do a final draft . . . but the most curious thing about this business is that they're typewritten. This is almost equivalent to telling me that he doesn't want to publish them. I don't know if he'll get over this *attack*. I now address myself to him as though to an editor. Because even if it's just the book of *Songs* I want to publish it. Besides, it's not *gypsy*. I hope everything will turn out right. After all, if I try to publish it's only to please a few friends and nothing else. I'm not interested in seeing my poems definitively *dead* . . . that is to say published.

Your poems in *Litoral*, which I already knew, are prodigious. Each time your poetry, clean and beautiful (that's it), penetrates me more and more. Beautiful, filled with a divine emotion, completely *grasped* in its wholeness. I can recite your *décimas* to you *by heart*. I recite them here among friends and *they are moved*. I protest against those who label you as excessively *cerebral*. There is such an extraordinary natural fragrance in your poetry that, if *fully felt*, it can even possess the gift of tears. I wish I could express my admiration. The *only total* admiration, if not veneration, I feel toward anyone in the new literature.

[Drawing]

1.9.2.7.

Germaine.

I've just received a telegram from Emilio in which he asks me if, *at last*, I'll publish my *Songs*. Immediately I told him Yes (in the tone of [Eugenio d'] Ors).

I like this book. I dedicate it to you, [Pedro] Salinas, and to Melchorito [Fernández Almagro] although I shouldn't have dedicated anything to Melchorito because of that grotesque and falsely Granadan *silhouette* of the Federico of *Impressions and Landscapes*[1] he did in your *Verso y Prosa*.

In this book appear the poems for Teresita.

A book of friends. There are seventy songs, from 1921 to 1923. I believe they are now perfected. Last night I read all of them to my brother. They have a good, lyric atmosphere. Among them there is a portrait of Juan Ramón [Jiménez] that begins:

> In the infinite white
> snow, spikenard and saltpit,
> he lost his fantasy.

I've omitted certain rhythmic songs in spite of their successes because that's what Clarity demanded. The songs are girded to my body and I am *master* of the book. A bad poet . . . very well! but master of my bad poetry.

When will I see you, dear Jorge? Right now I have several lyric projects but I don't know into which ones I should sink my teeth first. The day we get together will be a great day for *readings*. Give affectionate regards to Juan Guerrero [Ruiz] to whom all of Spain's poets owe a debt of gratitude, and tell him that when I write something of my projected poem I will send it to him for his magazine.

To Germaine my purest affection, and lots of kisses to the children. *Adiós*. Write me quickly and don't *hold out* on me. Don't deprive me of the gift of your poems and your friendship.

A hug. (I've managed to liven up the letter with drawings.)

Federico

---

[1]*Impresiones y paisajes (Impressions and Landscapes)*: Lorca's first book, prose, published in 1918.

TO MELCHOR FERNANDEZ ALMAGRO

[Granada, January, 1927]

[Drawing: a chophouse]

Dear Melchorito:

As always I send you my most joyous and affectionate hug. Soon you'll receive my first book. Dedicated to you, [Pedro] Salinas and [Jorge] Guillén. My three weaknesses.

I want to go to Madrid to see if I can settle the matter of *Mariana Pineda*. I don't like the work at all; you know that. But for now it's the only serious pretext I have to go to Madrid. Can you write me a letter telling me that my departure is necessary and convenient? This is no lie. I must go. Right? Do it this way . . . if you wish. I'm not forcing you.

My books are about to be published. They will be a surprise to many. The cliché of my gypsiness has gotten around *too much,* but this book of songs, for example, is a sharp, serene lyrical effort and seems to have great poetry in it (in the sense of nobility and quality, not *value*). It's not a *gypsy* book. I'm pleased. I've eliminated the rhythmic songs in spite of their success, because I want everything to have the rarified air of the mountains.

I hope you'll like it. On the cover it bears the constellation of Lyra just as it appears on the astronomical charts. Don't say anything to anybody until the book is out. It's better . . . such is my *myth* of publications.

[Drawing: two lemons]

Melchorito: Is the Federico of *Impressions and Landscapes* and your charming silhouette the same Federico that drew the basket of flowers? No, it seems you've remembered 1918 too much.

Adiós. A big hug from yours always

Federico

Write immediately. *Adiós,* you rascal!

97

TO JOSE MARIA COSSIO

[January, 1927]

[Drawing: basket of fruit; a cup]

Dear Cossío:

Forgive my delay. In Granada we say "late, but on time." Do I
arrive at a propitious moment? Without answering you, I remembered you, dear cousin,[1] every day. Now I'm forgetting you
totally, until you write me again. Will you write me? I'm working a lot these days. In a short time you'll receive my book *Songs*.
I'm thinking of sending you a book for your library that contains
my drawings.

Your book on the bulls will be delightful I'm sure. Why don't
we do one now on *crimes*? Among the Spanish ballads there's an
admirable collection. Especially the music. In the *Song Book of
Salamanca*[2] there are popular crimes with a marvelous emotion.
I, in Granada, have a few gems. Are you going to give the music
to the ballads in your book? It would be delightful. The ballad
of Pepe-Hillo has several musical versions. The ballad of the bull
of Matilla de los Caños is magnificent and later on, in the past
century, various bullfight melodies were written in Málaga, with
a truly moving Andalusian flavor. What do you think?

I will write out my two ballads right away. The first, about
Antoñito el Camborio, came out with enormous errata in
Litoral—an admirable magazine from Málaga. That's why I'm
copying out the image of the bullfighter again here. I'm sending
the one about Mariana Pineda in its entirety. I've put in a
Cayetano without even knowing who he is! Nor does it matter
to me, but it's a delightful name!

[Drawing: bullfighter. With the dedication: "To José María
Cossío. Federico García Lorca, 1927."]

I hope you don't resent me for having behaved so rudely.
You're too kind to behave as badly as I.

I hope you'll write me and we'll be friends as always. Here's an affectionate embrace from your friend

Federico García Lorca

[Drawing: two lemons]

---

[1] "Cousin" is used as a term of endearment. Cossío was a member of the Spanish Academy and the foremost writer on the art of bullfighting of this period.
[2] Folkloric poems and songs collected by Dámaso Ledesma.

TO MELCHOR FERNANDEZ ALMAGRO

[Granada, February, 1927]

Dear Melchor:

I've read that you're going from *La Epoca* to *La Voz*. Should I congratulate you? I don't know under what conditions you switched your store of talent, but I like the newspaper better. Before none of us could read your chronicles, and now we'll have the pleasure of savoring them. And of course, they'll be more effective. Here the common people of Granada have talked about this as your *triumph*. That putrid [Francisco Martínez] Lumbreras has opened his asshole mouth in your honor. You came, you struggled, and you conquered. People also say: "In *no time* flat that guy's going to kick out *Fabián Vidal* [Enrique Fajardo] and we'll have him as boss of *La Voz*." These Jew-Galicians in Granada are the worst in the world.

I'd like to leave right away, but my family fears the flu. Don't you think it's run its course?

Of course, I'm already sure that Xirgu won't be presenting the *by now famous* Mariana. Because I haven't gotten the least bit of news from her. Don't you think it's a bit strange? Because if she wants to do the premiere she should have shown some signs of life by now. If by any chance you should see her, ask her one more time.

Don't forget to respond in a long letter to everything I've said and asked. You write me the shortest letters all the time, and that's because you hardly love me any more.

Adiós, Melchorito. Here's a hug from

Federico

TO JORGE GUILLEN

[Granada, mid-February, 1927]

FIRST LETTER

Dear Jorge:

I'm sending you these poor things. You *choose* and publish whichever you wish. Once you have published them, RETURN THEM TO ME. Will you do it, [Juan] Guerrero [Ruiz]? Yes. Good.

They are bad things. At times I despair. I see that I'm not fit for anything. They are things from 1921. From 1921, when I was a child. Perhaps someday I will be able to express the extraordinary *real* drawings that I dream. Now I have a long way to go.

I'm far away.

Jorge, write me. Tell Teresita that I'm going to tell her the story of the little hen with the trailing dress and yellow hat. The rooster has a very big hat for rainy weather. Tell her that I'll tell her the story of the frog that played the piano and sang when given little cakes. And lots more.

Adiós. A hug from

Federico
(least of poets in the world,
but your friend)

SECOND LETTER

Dear Jorge:

The fellows in Granada are going to do a literary supplement for the local paper, *Defensor de Granada,* with the title *El gallo del Defensor.* It's illustrated by Dalí. Falla's publishing a magnificent article in it. Send something. Whatever you wish. For the first issue. Look how many things I've sent you.

Right now I'm terrified and weighted down by something superior to my strength. It seems that [Margarita] Xirgu is going to premiere *Mariana Pineda* (a romantic drama). Writing a romantic drama was fine three years ago. Now I see it as *peripheral* to my work. I don't know.

[Drawing of a rooster]

> Send me
> poetry or
> prose.
> Cock a doodle doo.

We're very busy now with this *rooster,* and we're hoping for success.

I'm *crazy* with happiness. Don't say anything to anybody. But my brother Paquito is writing a *marvelous* novel. Just that: marvelous. And it's nothing like any of my things. It's delightful. Don't say anything yet. It will be a tremendous surprise. I'm not blinded by the infinite love I have for him. No. It's a reality. I'm telling you this because you're so much a part of *me.* It's a release for my happiness. My brother was inhibited by my personality (you understand). He couldn't blossom next to me, because my impulse and my art scared him a bit. He had to get away, travel, meet the world on its own terms. But there it is. The poor guy is studying for a professional position in I don't know what field of law and he'll succeed so as not to displease my parents. He's a great student and he's a *protégé* of the entire faculty of the University. But what a great man of letters! He is destined to surpass those now writing. Last night I was comparing his prose and his style with that of [Pedro] Salinas and [Benjamín] Jarnés, just to give you highly regarded modern examples, and he has a distinct charm, *clearer* and more youthful than theirs. Besides, it's a *long novel* he's writing. A novel imbued with the Mediterranean Sea. Listen, he's written a chapter on a beauty contest at the baths of Málaga which is stupendous. This is one of the surprises. He's going to start to write for *El gallo.* And so will Enrique Gómez Arboleya, sixteen years old, who's written a story, *Lola y Lola,* delightful. The ineffable child whom we call *Don Luis Pitín* will also be writing stories of witches and sprites, the most imaginative you can imagine, and others who are just as good.

Among all of them, your poetry! Let's have that joy of rhythm and verse to enrich and *crown* the magazine!

I hope that *Verso y Prosa* and *El gallo* will be the closest of friends and love each other. You will beat our *drum,* and we'll proclaim in capital letters: Read *Verso y Prosa!* The only thing that frightens me is that everything I say seems marvelous to them and that's not good.

Adiós, Jorge. Regards to [Juan] Guerrero [Ruiz] and confer on him (in my name and that of the magazine) the shield of Alhamar!

A big hug. Answer me, man. Answer me. It's not right that you should write to [Fernando García] Vela who is a putrid Ortegista, and not to me. That displeases me. I'm not intelligent. That's true! But I am a poet.

Federico

Germaine, when are you coming to Granada? Why not this Carnival? Everybody gets together on the main street to see the masquerades, and the best of Granada is on its own and *on fire.* It would be delightful, because you'd be able to catch, on the sly, the ultimate enchantment of the city.

TO JORGE GUILLEN

[February 14, 1927]

My dear Jorge:

Today I'm tearing up a long letter of *complaints* that I wrote you. I receive your letters with the greatest joy. A letter from the poet of the best *verses*. I will do what you want. Tomorrow I'll send you poems and write to Dalí asking for a drawing.

By now the presses are *groaning* with my book of *Songs*. A book of surprises for many and of joy for a few. To Teresita I dedicate the song of the lizard and his wife because she will laugh a lot to see them cry (poor dears!).

I know that you'll keep this book in your house and cherish it. That is why I'm publishing it. My friends will receive it in a way that really moves me. Here in Granada all the fellows are preparing a party for the day the book arrives, and there will be music and dancing. Few books are received like this. But at heart I believe they are not receiving my poetry . . . they are receiving me.

I've gone through veritable anguish arranging the songs, but they are done! I'm sure of that. The book, good or bad, is of completely *noble* blood.

What a lovely ballad you've published. You sent it to me before. It has, like everything of yours, the grace and *modesty* of a nude statue.

There is in all your poetry an emotion, a GRIEF (yes, grief!) like the processional virgin's that overcomes its almost astronomical perfection.

Right now I'm writing a "Solitude" that, as you know, I began a long time ago. It's what I'm sending to the homage to Góngora . . . if it turns out well. Look at a few verses. Tell me what you think.

ANXIOUS SOLITUDE

NIGHT

Night of closed flower and hidden vein.
—Unripe almond green to the touch—
Night cut down too soon

stirred leaves and souls.
A mute fish in the water's clamorous expanse
lewdly bathed in the trembling,
luminous ivory, recently cut
from the adolescent horn of the moon.
And if the centaur on its banks
sings a delicious song of chase and arrows,
light green waves cull its accents,
the spikenards of never ending sorrow.
Lyra danced in the feigned curve,
immobile target of frozen geometry.
Wolf eyes sleep in the shadow
relinquishing the blood of the lamb.
On the opposite side, Philomel sings,
humid songs of ivy and hyacinth,
airborne plaint of the mad South,
over the fixed flute of the fountain.
While in the middle of the dark horror
feigning song and awaiting fear
a shipwrecked sailor's disquieting voice rang out:

This is a fragment. I still have to do a lot of work. Or maybe I'll throw it into the wastebasket. It's so difficult to get it right.

If you'd like, I could send you something closer to my own style. Don't get the wrong idea! I mean in the sense of something more *flexible*.

Here's another fragment:

Lilies of foam hundreds and hundreds of stars
descended to the absence of the waves.
Silk on drum, the sea stretched tight,
while Favonius dreams and Thetis sings.
Words of crystal and dark breeze,
roundly, yes, the mute fish speak.
Academy, in the cloister of the rainbow
beneath the dense and penetrable ecstasy.
A barbarous bridge of dolphins arrives
and the water turns into butterflies,
necklace of tears over the fine sands,
flying towards the armless hills.

The *Solitude* begins like this:

The moon rolls frozen, when Venus
with her salty skin, opens on the sand,

white pupils of innocent shells.
The night recovers its precious tracks
with sandals of phosphorus and foam.
While the stiff pulseless giant
scrapes its warm smooth back.
The night exalts its blurred scar.
On seeing its flesh converted into flesh
that shares in the hard star
and the mollusk without limits of fear.

· ·
· ·

Isn't it true that this is a pretty allusion to the myth of Venus? And I like this because it's true. "The mollusk without limits of fear."

Tell me what you think of these verses. And tell me soon. I'm working a lot and I believe I might not be able to finish this *Solitude*. On the other hand, it seems an irreverence that I should have to *force myself* to do this homage. I'm not sure.

Tomorrow I'll send you verses, but answer me. And I'll also be sending you money (how embarrassing!).

Good-bye. Affectionate regards to our beloved Guerrero.

Kisses to the children. Regards (my best and highest) to Germaine, and *for you* a very strong embrace from

Federico

Dalí's address is:
Monturiol 24
Figueras
Prov. de Gerona

TO JOSE BERGAMIN

[Granada, February, 1927]

[Drawing in color: fruit basket with oranges]

Dear Bergamín:

I've owed you a letter for many months. And I didn't write for the simple reason that I thought of you constantly. It was difficult for me to rend the silent veil that absence sets up between people, where memory so perfectly stylizes yesterday's handshakes and smiles.

I was confident of your unfailing friendship and that was enough. Today, besides greeting you affectionately, I have *to ask you a favor*. But don't be frightened.

The fellows in Granada (among whom are two positive *surprises* and one of them is a *novelist*) are going to do a literary supplement to the *Defensor de Granada* titled *El gallo del Defensor* and it's everybody's wish that you collaborate on it. Falla has already written a delightful article for the first number and it is necessary that you write or send a work of yours with all haste. This issue *will not come out* without your participation.

Today you are one of the most *beloved* of the young Andalusians and it's important that you be *generous* with them.

Gallo is illustrated by Dalí and in it, as I mentioned, two new people in whom I have absolute faith will make their debut, a poet and a *novelist*. Within three years you'll remember what I'm saying now. Why not do a few *"commissioned* aphorisms on the sultan rooster"? The plasticity of your talent goes well with the theme. The rooster is a subtle theme, a theme of daybreak which can never grow old. The rooster instinct is so sharpened and perfect that it ends up being a mechanism. Put a sultan rooster on top of your writing desk (almost, almost like an Andalusian horse). And if its steel tail feathers bring to mind Spanish fanfare, its pure breast, on the other hand, bursts over *virgin* lands and waters, while its cockcrow shoots an intelligent rocket of dark light at the people's stupid torpor.

We await you. We don't want to see you with a quill in your hat, like a Swiss hunter. We want to see you with a rooster in your hand, so schematic, perfect and joyful that it resembles a pair of deluxe *banderillas*.

The day before yesterday we read "Don Lindo of Almería" in the company of [Antonio] Luna [García], my brother and other friends. I liked it very much. But it shouldn't be called "Don Lindo of Almería," but "Don Lindo of Cádiz." The whole ballet has a delicious *colonial* air of seaside Cádiz. Ironically, one must recall the rhythm of the *habanera* in order to understand it. Almería has a harshness and a dusty Algerian saffron that doesn't fit in with the features of the last *farce* which you've drawn so well. Cádiz, on the other hand, can glorify its parrots and palm trees to the point where the seventeenth century says enough. The plasticity of the ballet is so magnificent. But the music that it needs, in my judgment, is a music without *marrow*, an *exterior* music like a golden and empty shell. Music for the eyes, with those drumbeats that vibrate vaguely in the kidneys. I was extraordinarily entertained by the hyperbolic parrot, carnation, and St. Anthony, and it's a pleasure to tell you this.

Adiós. Send your work quickly.

An affectionate and Andalusian hug from your friend

Federico

[Your house]: Acera del Casino, 31.

Soon I'll be seeing you in Madrid.

Let's see if this year we can get together and you'll stop thinking of me as a *gypsy;* you don't know how much this myth hurts me and how *false* it is in its essence, although it may not appear so in its form. See you soon and *write me*.

TO JORGE GUILLEN

[Granada, March, 1927]

[Postcard]

[Jorge Guillén, Capuchinas, 6. Murcia.]

Dear Jorge:

How beautifully *Verso y Prosa* came out this month! Lovely.
Guillermo's [de Torre] article is nice and it pleased me, although
I don't deserve so much. It eulogizes me so much that I don't
recognize myself.

I had a long letter about poetry ready for you. I tore it up. I
realize that I'm very closely *tied* to other poets and that my outcry would be *terrible.* But what a pure and poetic outcry! *Ay!*
dear Jorge, we're going down two wrong roads: one leads to
Romanticism and the other towards the snakeskin and the *ci-
cada's* empty shell. *Ay!* What deceit! It's sad. But I've got to keep
still. To speak would create a *scandal.* These days I'm reading
just *empty poetry* or decorative nonsense, like one newly bap-
tized. I keep quiet. Forgive me . . . but I have to hold hand
over mouth in order to keep quiet. *Adiós.* Give my best regards
to [Juan] Guerrero [Ruiz]. Love to your children and Germaine
and an effusive embrace of poetic communion from

Federico

I'm slightly ill and can't go to Madrid as yet. Write quickly.

ANA MARIA DALI

[May or June, 1927]

Dear Ana María:

Affectionate greetings from Barcelona. The child's [Salvador Dalí] decorations are delightful. How do you say *"nublo"*? And a little spoon? Tell Consuelo not to raise such a racket in the kitchen—it stops me from writing. Give lots of kisses to the little bear.[1] Four days ago I found him smoking a cigar near the Columbus Monument.

Adiós, Ana María. I'll be happy to hear that your aunt is in better health. Give her regards in my name. Regards from

Federico.

Señorita Ana Mariquita Dalí

Playa de Llené
Cadaqués
Prov. de Gerona

---

[1] The "little bear" was a stuffed bear who "lived" at the Dalí residence in Cadaqués but who (from Lorca's correspondence) sometimes seemed to have an independent existence.

TO MELCHOR FERNANDEZ ALMAGRO

[Cadaqués, July, 1927]

Dear Melchor:

I'm going to be a nuisance. I'd like to know how I can collect from the Society of Authors and if you can collect it and send it to me. Is it a bother? Pardon me, Melchorito, but you're the only one I can tell this to in confidence and can ask to do me this favor.

Answer me by return mail. I don't want to ask my family for traveling money now since I've already spent an awful sum.

Cadaqués is stupendous and it's a real delight to live here, but my family calls me back urgently, with reason. It will be difficult to leave and I'm waging a real battle with the Dalí family, but I have no choice.

I've worked a lot on new and original poems, belonging, now that I've finished the *Gypsy Ballads,* to another *class of things.* You've written me very little, and this makes me think that you're keeping me at arm's length and that you're worse than a *rogue. Adiós,* Melchorito. Answer me and receive a close embrace from

Federico

TO MANUEL DE FALLA

[July, 1927]

My dear Don Manuel:

When you receive this letter I'll be on the road to Granada after leaving—with a certain regret—this very beautiful Catalonian land where I've had such a nice time. You can't imagine how much they love you here and how much attention I've had lavished on me only because of the fact that I'm a friend of yours.

I thought of you constantly while the decor for *María Pineda* was being prepared, full of a marvelous Andalusianism sagaciously intuited by Dalí by way of genuine photographs and my exalted discourse, hours and hours and without a touch of *localism*. We'll be speaking about all this and about various plans I have which might arouse your interest.

The "Sacramental plays" have been a great success at last *all over Spain* and a success for our friend [Hermenegildo] Lanz, who day after day succeeds with modesty in winning our utmost admiration. This makes me extraordinarily happy and demonstrates the many things that can be done and *which we must* do in Granada. Greet María del Carmen on my behalf, thank her for the postcard and for you an embrace of respectful affection and admiration.

Federico

I was *compelled* by everyone to put on an exhibition of drawings. And I sold four! I'm sending you a catalog as a souvenir. A thousand thanks for everything and for your congratulations. Greeting you affectionately.

TO ANA MARIA DALI

[August, 1927]

[Drawing: Enriqueta's melancholy]

Dear Ana María:

I've been in Granada for several days now and every moment I must paint your portrait for my sisters who ask about you constantly.

I had such a good time in Cadaqués it seems as though I've had a happy dream. Especially waking up to encounter "that" which one sees from the *window*.[1] My good angels happened to be the delightful parishioner Salvador de Horta and Puig y Pujades who presented it. I can now recall the tiniest detail of my stay in your house, and I ask you on my knees to forgive me for little things that by chance might not have been quite right, like my *grave* throat illness which caused you so much trouble.

Here the doctor has looked me over and said that it was a bit of pharyngitis that, although bothersome, is of no consequence. Enrique had already told me that.[2] Right now, as you know, I'm in the Huerta de San Vicente [family house], near Granada, and in a few days we're going to the mountains of Lanjarón, and after that to Málaga to round off the summer. I'm feeling fine here. The house is big and surrounded by water and corpulent trees, *but that's not the whole truth.* Here there exists an incredible amount of *historical melancholy* that makes me look back toward the fair and neutral atmosphere of your terrace, into which, at times, Lydia shoots a jet of strong pepper which brings out the visible flavor of the air even more. I have received *L'Amic de les Arts* and saw your brother's prodigious poem ["San Sebastián"]. Here in Granada we've translated it and it has created an extraordinary impression. Especially on my brother, *who wasn't expecting it,* in spite of what I told him. It's simply a matter of a new prose replete with unsuspected relationships and very subtle *points of view.*

From here it acquires a charm and an intelligent light that redoubles my admiration.

I'm starting to work (on very bad things, naturally), but they distract me and gladden this emphatic monotony in which I find myself. I hope you write me giving me news of all that is happening in Cadaqués and how the sea is doing and if María, Eduard and the petite Margarita are well. Give my affectionate regards to Rosita and sing in my name *"una vez un Choralindo . . . etc."* Toss corn to the geese!

Regards to Raimunda.

Adiós, Ana María: The little bear sent me a card telling me all sorts of things about [Eduardo] Marquina and saying that you've almost forgotten me, and that he can't forget me because of his admiration for me and for the nice way I treated him.

Within a few days I'll send him a walking stick. Please tell him that.

Regards to your brother the little fool (you know?).

Regards to your father and for you the best regards and affection of your *ami*

Federico

Write me and tell me what your brother is painting. Send me the photos! Don't you want to?

---

[1] "That" refers to the view of the sunrise over the Mediterranean from his bedroom window.
[2] The Dalí's gardener.

TO SEBASTIAN GASCH

[Granada, August, 1927]

My dear Gasch:

It is absolutely necessary that I give you a check so that you may pick up from the station (Great Velocity) an embrace of mine that I forward to you conveniently packed in a little Venetian crystal box. I like your article[1] and thank you profusely for it. You already know what extraordinary pleasure I feel at being treated like a painter.

But now I'm starting to write and illustrate poems like this one that I'm sending dedicated to you. When a subject is too lengthy or contains a poetically stale emotion, I resolve it with drawing pencils. This makes me very happy and is extraordinarily amusing. The magazine gets better each time and each time will be more successful. There's hardly anyone in Granada, but I will take care of the subscriptions in due order. Tell me where I should remit the proceeds of the subscriptions.

In our circle of friends it has made a magnificent impression and my brother is enthusiastic.

How admirable the *San Sebastián* of Dalí! It's one of the most intense poems that one can read. In this fellow, in my opinion, is to be found the greatest glory of the *eternal Catalonia*. I'm preparing a study of him which you'll translate into Catalonian, if you wish, and I'll publish it first in that language.

I remember you often and will be overjoyed if you write me as soon as possible. Although I sent you a card the other day, I want to thank you today, and ask you to pick up that embrace at the station of the four Seasons[2] of the calendar. Be hearing from you.

Federico

---

[1] Gasch's article *"Una exposiciò i un decorat"* ("An exhibition and a decoration") appeared in the July 31, 1927, issue of *L'Amic de les Arts*.
[2] A play on the word *"estación"* which means season as well as station.

TO SEBASTIAN GASCH

[ca. August, 1927]

[Fragment]

In the midst of the Sierra Nevada one is in the *heart of the soul* of Africa. All the eyes are by now perfectly African, with a ferocity and poetry that can hold off the Mediterranean. This tree— the postcard depicts the "fat chestnut" of Lanjarón—will give you an idea of the vegetation and rich quality of the water. Here you understand the wounds of St. Roque, the tears of blood, and the taste for the buried knife. Strange and Berberesque Andalusia.

TO SEBASTIAN GASCH

[Summer, 1927?]

[Fragment]

My dear friend Sebastián:

In effect, you're right in everything you say. But my state is not one of "perpetual dream." I've expressed myself badly. Some days I've skirted the dream, but haven't fallen totally into it, possessing, of course, a tether of laughter to hang on to and a secure wooden scaffold. I never venture into territories alien to man, because I beat a fast retreat and almost always rip up the fruits of my voyage. When I do a purely abstract thing, it always has (I believe) a safe conduct pass of smiles and a rather human equilibrium . . .

My state is always happy, and this dreaming of mine is not dangerous for me, because I have defenses; it is dangerous for one who lets himself be fascinated by the great dark mirrors that poetry and madness wield at the bottom of their chasms. I HAVE AND I FEEL I HAVE MY FEET FIRMLY ON THE GROUND IN ART. I FEAR the abyss and the dreams in the reality of my life, in love, in the daily encounter with others. And that really is terrible and fantastic.

[1927?]

[Fragment]

Everyday I appreciate Dalí's talent even more. He seems to me unique and he possesses a serenity and a *clarity* of judgment about whatever he's planning to do that is truly moving. He makes mistakes and it doesn't matter. *He's alive.* His denigrating intelligence unites with his disconcerting childishness, in such an unusual combination that it is absolutely captivating and original. What moves me most about him now is his *fever* of constructions (that is to say, creation), in which he tries to create out of *nothing* with such strenuous efforts and throws himself into the gales of creativity with so much faith and so much intensity that it seems incredible. Nothing more dramatic than this objectivity and this search for happiness for happiness' sake. Remember that this has always been the Mediterranean canon. "I believe in the resurrection of the flesh," says Rome. Dalí is the man who struggles with a golden ax against phantoms. "Don't speak to me of supernatural things. How repulsive is Santa Catalina!" says Falla.

> Oh straight line!
> Pure lance without a knight!
> How my twisted path
> dreams of your light!

Say I. But Dalí doesn't let himself be led. Besides his faith in astral geometry, he needs to be at the helm. It moves me; Dalí inspires the same pure emotion (and may God Our Father forgive me) as that of the baby Jesus abandoned on the doorstep of Bethlehem, with the germ of the crucifixion already latent beneath the straws of the cradle.

TO SEBASTIAN GASCH

[Lanjarón, August or September, 1927]

[Fragments]

I thank you profusely for your praise, but it helps me to draw like you have no idea, and I really enjoy myself with the drawings. I *propose* themes to myself before drawing and achieve the *same* effects as when I'm not thinking about anything. Naturally, on these occasions I find myself with an almost physical sensation that carries me to levels where it's difficult to find one's footing and where one almost flies over the abyss. It takes a lot out of me to keep up a normal conversation with these people at the spa [of Lanjarón], because my eyes and my words are someplace else. They are in the immense library that no one has read, in the freshest air, a country where things dance on one foot.

. . . .

These last drawings I've done cost me a great deal of time and effort. I abandoned my hand to virgin territory and my hand together with my heart brought to light the miraculous elements. I discovered them and took them down. I put out my hand again, and so, out of many elements, I chose the characteristics of the subject or the prettiest and most inexplicable ones, and I composed my drawing. This is how I composed the "Sevillian Ireso," [1] the "Mermaid," the "St. Sebastian," and almost all of those that have a little cross. There are pure miracles, like "Cleopatra," that gave me a shiver when that harmony of lines appeared which *I hadn't thought of, nor dreamed, nor desired; I wasn't even inspired,* and I said, "Cleopatra!" on seeing it, and that's the truth! Later my brother corroborated it. Those lines were *the exact portrait, the pure emotion* of the Queen of Egypt. Some drawings come out like that, like the most beautiful metaphors, and others by searching for them in the place *where one knows for sure* they're to be found. It's like fishing. Sometimes the fish goes into the basket by itself and other times one chooses the likeliest waters and throws in the best hook to catch it. The hook is called *reality.* I've thought about and produced these little drawings with a poetic-plastic or plastic-poetic criterion, in fitting union. And many are lineal metaphors or sublimated commonplaces, like the "St. Sebastian" and the "Peacock." I've tried to choose the essential features of form and emotion, or of super-reality or super-form, to turn them into a *symbol* that, like a magic key, might help us *better understand* the reality that they possess in the world.

[1] The drawing has been lost and the title is obscure.

TO SEBASTIAN GASCH

[August or September, 1927]

[Fragments]

But *without torture or dream* (I detest the art of dreams), or complications. These drawings are pure poetry or pure plasticity at the same time. I feel clean, comforted, happy, *a child* when I do them. And I am horrified by the *word* that I have to use to name them. I'm horrified by the painting that they call *direct,* which is nothing but an anguished struggle with forms in which the painter is *always* vanquished and the work is *dead.* In these abstractions I see *created* reality joining itself to the reality that surrounds us like the real clock is attached to the concept the way a barnacle is to a rock. You're right, my dear Gasch, one must connect abstractions. What's more, I would call these drawings you'll be receiving (I'm sending them registered), *Very Human Drawings.* Because almost all of them pierce the heart with their little arrows.

. . . .

As you probably know, I returned from Lanjarón and I'm once more in the Huerta de San Vicente in bucolic surroundings, eating exquisite fruits and singing on the swing with my brother and sisters all day long and fooling around so much, that at times I'm embarrassed because of my age.

TO ANA MARIA DALI

[November, 1927]

Dear friend Ana Patera y Seachera de Cuca:[1]

I received your dear photos and your pretty drawings while laid up in bed.

I've been very sick for four days with a temperature of *101 degrees*. I've had food poisoning, and thank God I didn't die, but I've been very ill. Today, seated in bed, I'm writing to give you thanks, sweet little thanks, and to send you this photo of my sisters. They don't show up well, but one can recognize them. They've autographed it for you.

I can't write much because my head is spinning. I do this as proof of my affection and friendship, *pirulita*.

I'll answer Sir Little Bear [Eduardo] Marquina very shortly.

He's extremely cute.

Adiós, until I get better, when I'll write you again. Lots of affection from your friend, *seachero,*

Federico

[1] Lorca often invented whimsical names and nonsensical rhymes.

TO MELCHOR FERNANDEZ ALMAGRO

[Granada, January, 1928]

Dear Melchor:

This is the stationery of the Granadan fellows' new magazine. The drawing is by Dalí. I haven't written you because I have been busy writing many new things which you'll be seeing. But naturally I can't forget you and I read your delightful articles in *La Voz* without missing one. The one you did on Guerrero[1] was a model of feeling and elegance.

Your article goes, naturally, in the first issue. It's a magazine of Granadans and only Granadans. So that if others publish in it, they will be appearing as guests.

If you wish to correct something in your article tell us immediately, since the original is ready to go. I'm glad I stayed for a while, because the magazine is now under way.

I've finished *The Shoemaker's Prodigious Wife;* I'm working on the "Ode to the Holy Sacrament" and preparing the lecture I have to give at the Residencia de Estudiantes, which will be on the "Pathos of the Spanish Lullaby," a difficult topic, because there's nothing written on this and one faces infinite problems and conflicts that are difficult to resolve.

I expect to go to Madrid right away, where we'll talk about everything we have on our hands.

Ah perfidious Melchorante!

Write me and give me news of Madrid. Greetings to our friends, and especially to [Francisco] Ayala and [Miguel] P[érez] Ferrero, who meet with you in the afternoons at the Granja [café].

Ayala, as a Granadan, must contribute often. Tell him I'll be writing him.

Adiós, dear Melchorito. A very affectionate embrace from

Federico

---

[1] The actress María Guerrero, whose obituary Melchor Fernández Almagro wrote.

[Granada, January 20, 1928]

My dear Gasch:

It's in Granada that I'm really at ease and open to the delicious appreciation of friendship. I was certainly right not to go to Barcelona. I wouldn't have enjoyed it and besides we wouldn't have *been together*. Now if at last I do go, on my own, we'll be better off.

You have no idea with what willingness I'd go and, you can be sure, if I don't go it won't be my fault, but the fault of *Destiny*, or a contrary wind from which none is free.

If Dalí finishes his service soon, it will be wonderful to be together. I'm finishing up my business and, God willing, I'll succeed in getting to Barcelona. As you know, my *Romancero* is ready. If I can, I'll bring you the copies myself.

Barcelona attracts me because of all of you.

You know perfectly that we see eye to eye and that our conversations are mutually beneficial. I always say that you're the only critic and the only perspicacious person I've met and that there's not another fellow in Madrid of your class and artistic knowledge, nor, naturally enough, of your sensibility. Therefore I don't think you ought to have any reservations about your articles (always graceful and extremely useful) in the *Gaceta literaria*.

Your work is badly needed and you should publish much more. As for your Castilian, I assure you that it's noble and correct and fulfills the end to which you utilize it. But much more important than the language you use are your ideas, your manner of exposition and your sureness of technique in judging. You shouldn't ever harbor this thought. Your Castilian is good and will get progressively better as you publish more. I think it would be a good idea for you to publish a book on modern painting. This will open up large areas for you in Spain and America, an area into which you ought to expand and in which sure success awaits you.

Very rarely do I err in these matters of *intuition*.

And in Madrid, dear Sebastián, you're needed more than in

Barcelona, because Madrid is pictorially the seat of all the rotten and abominable, although literarily speaking it is very good and is taken into account now in Europe, as you very well know.

As for publishing my drawings, I'm quite decided. In Barcelona perhaps I'll publish them at less cost. I'd like you to find out exactly how much it would cost. I would publish almost all the ones I sent you plus a few more. I'll intersperse some poems and Dalí, as well, will include his drawings and also some poems.

You would compose a prologue or study, and we would try to see to it that the book circulates. Tell me if you like this project which we could make still better.

I'd like very much to do this because it would be a beautiful book of poems.

I'll be sending you a drawing for the magazine.

Here in Granada the young group's magazine is being published at last with the title of *gallo*. I think highly of these fellows. Actually, I'm of the opinion that they should do it exclusively by themselves in order to do something in which our names don't appear, since they're everywhere already. Send us a *valiant* new article on new art, which could be accompanied by two or three photos or drawings. We have a great deal of trouble with money and won't be able to thank you with more than affection, gratitude and good will.

Adiós. Here's a strong embrace from

Federico

Regards to our friends.

TO SEBASTIAN GASCH

[Granada, March, 1928]

My very dear Sebastián:

By now you've probably received *gallo.* I've not written to you previously because I've worked a lot to get this magazine under way. As I'm its father, I can't judge it. It's dear to me. And, of course, I believe it's the *liveliest* among the young reviews. It has, I think, *unity* and personality. Tell me what you think of it. We're getting lots of very favorable opinion, thank God. *Objectively,* I find faults, but they'll be corrected in time. We thank you from our hearts for the article on Picasso. Thanks, Sebastián! You've done well with this admirable address on our great artist.

In Granada *gallo* has caused a real scandal. Granada is a literary city and nothing *new* ever happened to her. So that you can't imagine what a stir *gallo* has created. Within two days the edition was exhausted and today people are paying double the price for a copy. There was a big fight at the University yesterday between "Gallistas" and "anti-Gallistas," and in cafés, clubs, and houses it's the talk of the town. I'll be telling you more about it. We're now preparing the second issue. Your article heads it off, naturally. You'll always have the place of honor wherever I may be. And now . . . a hug for the manifesto! *gallo* adheres to it in the second issue and we're working on a commentary of it. Embrace my dear [Luis] Montanyá and tell him I've lost his address. That he should send it to me. To you I say that the manifesto is joyous, brave, *alive,* full of grace and *truth.*

I have to thank you again and again. Thanks for your elegant article in the *Gaceta.*[1] You're overwhelming me. I don't know how I'll ever be able to repay your kind treatment of me. It's too much. I can only repay you by putting the little talent I have at your disposal. Thanks. It's not right, dear Gasch, to put my absurd name among so many illustrious ones. You shouldn't have done that.

I'm definitely publishing my drawings. Do the prologue for them.

A heartfelt embrace from

Federico

My regards to all our friends. And hurrah to the *L'Amic de les Arts* for their marvelous October issue. Hurrah!

---

[1] Gasch's article *"Lorca, dibujante"* ("Lorca, Draftsman") appeared in the March 15, 1928, issue of the *Gaceta literaria*.

TO SEBASTIAN GASCH

[Granada, March, 1928]

My dear Gasch:

Many thanks for your letter, always so eagerly awaited and well-received. All my friends are extremely thankful for your praise and thankful for your cooperation. A thousand thanks. How can we be less than happy if you're going to contribute to every issue? Prepare and send your manuscript for *gallo* number three. You should do a nice job with reproductions of whatever you wish. Don't worry about length. You have a great obligation to *explicate* and encourage the art of our epoch.

We'll send you the Picassos as soon as we get them from Madrid, where they are making the reproductions to size. In this number my brother makes his *debut* as a writer with a prose piece that is splendid, it is so purely Latin, purely Mediterranean.

We're going to be starting immediately on the edition of *Paradise Closed To Many, Gardens Open To Few,* of our Soto de Rojas. We can make a great book and we will.

You already know that I am definitely going to publish my drawings in an edition put out by *gallo*. I want them to be accompanied by an essay of yours and another of Dalí's. Prologue and epilogue. I sent Dalí four of my drawings in the last couple of days. Tell him to send them to you if you want some for *L'Amic de les Arts*.

Write me. We'll put a commentary on your manifesto in *gallo*. Andalusia and Catalonia are joined by *gallo* and *L'Amic de les Arts,* although there are people who rage, kick, and would like to devour us.

Dalí (naturally) thinks *gallo* is horrible and says that his *San Sebastián* is horrendous. That I knew in advance. His letter is delightful and we died laughing at his silliness. But he is absolutely wrong. He's unjust. And unreasonable. You can't bring the criteria of the plastic arts to literary art. In this he's admirable, but he is very wrong.

Adiós, Sebastián. Here's an affectionate embrace from

Federico

TO JORGE GUILLEN

[Granada, March 24, 1928]

[Mr. Jorge Guillén, Capuchinas, 6. Murcia.]

Dear Jorge:

What's wrong? What are you up to? Your friend the painter was here, but I still hadn't received your letter, and he made a very strange face when I told him you hadn't written me. I tried to be nice to him and I was *even excessive* in my welcoming and friendly manner; but the man left me, and when I offered my services in accompanying him, he told me: "I am a wanderer. I have no home." And off he went. In short, my brother and I were very perplexed. Two days later I received your letter. I believe that that gentleman turned cool on finding out that I didn't know who he was, and didn't want anything further to do with me and my brother. I made every possible effort to be friendly; but he didn't even tell me *his name*. A very strange thing. I'm sending you a very big hug for your poem, which is superb. I'm sorry that you weren't able to publish the revised version, but it's nice that it turned out that way. What did you think of *gallo*? Tell me. We've sent you a special issue, without advertisements. Answer me. You don't know how much I would like to see you and to be with Teresita and Claudio. I'll no longer recognize them if I see them.

Oh, if I could go to Murcia, though it be on foot like that painter of yours! Write me a long letter, and I'll send you the *décimas* which I've dedicated to you. Regards to Germaine and the children.

For you a fraternal hug from

Federico

write me!

[Two photographs accompanied the letter. On the back of one photo he writes:]

Here I am high in the Alpujarras, where I went with two friends. By my side are the guides. The atmosphere is fantastic.

One never sees the Sierra Nevada. When will we go together to these places? One loses the idea of Europe. What's this? I'm serious in the photo because I'm pondering my surprise.

[And on the back of the other photograph:]

Here I am in Pitres, a village without voice or mountain doves. Crucified in the Y of the tree.

[Granada, April 7, 1928]

Dear Gasch:

Many thanks for your letters. Our heartfelt thanks for the idea of an issue dedicated to Andalusia. All Andalusia will thank you for it, and, of course, you can count on me. I'll look for advertisers and whatever is necessary here in Granada and wherever I can. As you can see, each day Andalusia and Catalonia are brought closer together, thanks to us. This is very important and they don't realize it, but later on they will. [Manuel de] Falla hasn't come yet, but he's about to arrive and will be as excited by the idea as we are. Falla is in love with Catalonia and will collaborate wholeheartedly. The issue can be a *glorious scandal.* I haven't written you sooner because of *gallo* and the divine Holy Week of Andalusia. *Gallo* is ready, but hasn't come out yet on account of the engravers. Your article leads off. In my opinion it's very beautiful and very bold. In this issue we're reproducing the *whole* manifesto and Joaquín Amigo Aguado, one of the most worthwhile young men in Granada, with great enthusiasm and integrity, comments on it with a eulogy of you three [Salvador Dalí, Sebastián Gasch, and Luis Montanyá].

As you'll see, your manifesto has had here the reception it deserved.

We're hoping you'll do us a favor. You'll receive six or seven reproductions of Manuel Angeles Ortiz and you'll do an essay on this painter for the next issue. *Manolo has never been talked about in Granada!* And he's been underestimated. It is our duty to talk about this great painter and friend. Since you'll be a regular writer, I'm asking you to do this. I hope you'll pursue it. You'll see that this is only proper. We'll put the article about Domingo in another issue. This is to fulfill an *obligation* with the review.

I believe you'll do this with the literary love which we put into our work. You already know the story of Manolo. I told you about that. How he left Granada with the yearning for purity and new horizons which this fellow always had.

A rather long essay. He is a disciple of Picasso. Probably the first and, certainly, the one Picasso likes most. You can deal, on the rebound, with Picasso's art. In short, dear Sebastián, whatever you want.

Soon you'll be getting *gallo*. Meanwhile, an affectionate embrace from

Federico

[Luis] Montanyá sent me an essay on the young poetry of Catalonia which we will publish *in toto* in the third issue. It's beautiful.

Regards to [Víctor] Sabater and [Manuel] Font.

Write me!

I hope you'll do the article with due speed.

TO JORGE ZALAMEA

[1928]

I would be sorry
if
you
were
miffed
at

the letter I sent you. Can't a poet scold his wayward friends?
Come now, I should hope so. It would be foolish. And you are
no fool. What do you know about what I'm feeling? I wouldn't
have been at ease without saying what I said.

But I showed you quite well that I wasn't angry.

Good-bye.

I'm working on a poem now called the "Academy of the Rose
and the Jar of Ink" [unpublished]. The poem is cruel, but clean.
Dalí is coming in September. In his last letter he told me: "You
are a Christian tempest and have need of my paganism. This past
season in Madrid you gave yourself to something you should
never have given yourself to. I'll come to get you to give you a
sea cure. It will be winter time and we will light a fire. The poor
beasts will be nearly frozen. You will remember that you are an
inventor of marvels and we'll live together with a camera."

He's like that, this marvelous friend.

Aren't you coming to Granada? Come!

Adiós. Another more heartfelt *adiós.*

Adiós.

And another from further off.

Fede
ri
co

TO SEBASTIAN GASCH

[Granada, September, 1928]

Dear Sebastián:

I received your letter with great happiness. My drawings are liked by a group of sensitive people, but they are very little known. I haven't been concerned about reproducing them and for me they are a private matter. If not for you, the Catalonians, I wouldn't have gone on drawing. I'm thinking of putting on an exhibition in Madrid. What do you say? And if I should do a book?

I want to send you some drawings and an unpublished poem for *L'Amic*. Is that all right?

I'm starting to work. I'm finishing up the "Ode to the Holy Sacrament of the Altar," which for me has great expressive force and an original and very new manner. I'm also composing the "Ode to Sesostris," the "Sardanápolos of the Greeks," full of humor, weeping and Dionysian rhythm.

I'm *vexed* and afflicted by passions which I have to vanquish, but I'm beginning to emerge, free, alone, in my own creation and effort. I'll be sending you parts of my new poems, and I expect that within two or three days you'll receive my book.

As for *gallo,* I want it to come out the minute I get to Granada. Send us the article on [Manuel] Angeles Ortiz.

And one more time, long live the *rooster*! We want to put out a number dedicated to Dalí. He's going to come to Granada and we owe him this homage. Advise him in your letters to come. Tell him that he needs to visit this important South, which is the truth.

You can't imagine how eagerly we wait for him.

My silence, dear Gasch, doesn't spring from my heart.

I don't forget you ever. You know that I have you in mind in everything I do.

Greetings to our friends; write me. And here's a strong embrace from

Federico

Greetings to your mother.

TO SEBASTIAN GASCH

[Granada, September, 1928]

My dear Sebastián:

Enclosed are the two poems.[1] I hope you like them. They answer to my new *spiritualist* manner, pure disembodied emotion, detached from logical control but—careful! careful!—with a tremendous poetic logic. It is not surrealism—careful!—the clearest self-awareness illuminates them.

They're the first I've done. Naturally, they're in prose because verse is a confinement they can't withstand. But in them you will find, naturally, my true heart's tenderness.

I am always grateful for your praise of my drawings. I must publish a book.

Convince Dalí that he should come to Granada.

I feel, as always, a great desire to go to Barcelona to be among you, with you, strolling along the Ramblas, through the marvelous port, through the picnic spots of Montjuit [*sic*], where we had such a good time.

Write me. Keep the drawings you published. My gift to you. And that way you can make a collection of silly trifles.

Adiós, Sebastián. Here's an affectionate hug from

Federico

---

[1] *"Suicidio en Alejandria"* ("Suicide in Alexandria") and *"Nadadora sumergida"* ("Swimmer Submerged").

TO SEBASTIAN GASCH

[Sierra Nevada (Granada), September 8, 1928]

Dear Gasch:

I went to the *sierra* and returned today. Forgive my belatedness. I haven't been to Granada for days. Today I sent out for envelopes in which to send you the Domingo photos, but there weren't any. I'll do it tomorrow. I'll also send you the Picassos. Forgive me.

I send along drawings. You're the only person for whom I do this since I feel you understand me very well.

If you wish, publish a few in *L'Amic*. And, of course, tell me what you think of them. With sincerity. We're enthusiastic about your article on Manuel Angeles [Ortiz], which is so very fine. Full of sound judgment, meditation, and harmony. And with that enthusiasm of yours, so admirable, that only genuine critics have, those who give battle and don't worry about pleasing everyone.

Thanks. We'll publish it with due care and perfection.

I'm working with great devotion on several things of very different genres. I'm composing all sorts of poems. I'll be sending some to you. If you like the drawings tell me which one or ones you'd like to publish and I'll send you their corresponding poems. I'll do it immediately.

Yesterday Dalí wrote me a long letter concerning my book [*Romancero gitano*]. (Have you gotten it yet? I sent it to you several days ago.) A sharp, arbitrary letter that sets forth an interesting poetic problem. Of course, the *putrefactos* do not understand my book, although they say that they do.

In spite of everything, it holds no interest for me any more, or hardly any. It died on my hands in the most tender way. My poetry takes an even keener flight. A personal turn it seems.

How I'd love to be with all of you.

Don't forget to tell Dalí to come to Granada. It's important we see each other for many reasons. Besides, we have to prepare a Dalí issue, and if we have money perhaps all of modern Catalonian and Andalusian painting. To show how only these two Mediterranean regions triumph on the peninsula.

Write me immediately.

Affectionate regards to all our friends. Tell Luis Montanyá I'll write him and ask if he got my book.

Adiós, Sebastián. Here's an affectionate embrace from your best

Federico

Reply!

TO SEBASTIAN GASCH

[1928?]

[Fragment]

The truth is what's alive and now they try to fill us up with deaths and cork dust. The absurd, if it's alive, is true; the theorem, if it's dead, is a lie. Let the fresh air in! Aren't you bothered by the idea of a sea with all its fish tied by little chains to one place, unknowing? I'm not disputing dogma. But dread the thought of where "that dogma" leads.

TO JORGE ZALAMEA

[September, 1928]

My dear Jorge:

At last I got your letter. I had already written you one and tore it up.

You must have had a bad summer. Fortunately, autumn, which gives me life, is already coming in. I too have had a bad time. Very bad. One needs to have the amount of happiness God bestowed on me in order not to succumb before the number of conflicts that have assaulted me lately. But God never abandons me. I've worked a lot and I'm working now. After constructing my "odes," in which I have so much hope, I'm closing this cycle of poetry to do something else. I am fashioning now a sort of VEIN-OPENING poetry, a poetry that has EVADED reality with an emotion reflecting all of my love of things and my mockery of things. Love of death and joking about death. Love. My heart. That's how it is.

All day I turn out poems like a factory. And then I go in for the manly, in the style of a pure Andalusian, to a bacchanal of flesh and laughter. Andalusia is incredible. Orient without poison, Occident without action. Each day I experience new surprises. The beautiful flesh of the South thanks you after you have stepped all over her.

In spite of everything, I'm neither well nor happy. Today is a FIRST CLASS gray day in Granada. From the Huerta de San Vicente (my mother's name is Vicenta) where I live, among magnificent fig trees and corpulent oaks, I behold the panorama of mountains that's the most beautiful (for its atmosphere) in Europe.

As you see, my dear friend, I write to you on *gallo* stationery, because now we have revived the magazine and we're composing the third issue.

I think it will be excellent.

Adiós, Jorge. Here's an affectionate embrace from

Federico

Try to be happy! It's necessary to be happy, a *duty* to be happy. Take it from me, I who am passing through one of the saddest and most unpleasant moments of my life.

Write me.

TO JORGE GUILLEN

[Granada, October or November, 1928]

My dear Jorge:

It's been two months since I've had my book wrapped up and ready to send to you. I am the height of laziness. But I always think of you as the best of the best, which you are.

I'd love with all my heart and soul to see you and exchange impressions on so many things that even two days wouldn't be enough. First of all, forgive me for that stupid telegram I sent.[1] Imprudent telegram that wasn't sent willingly, but was *Viñuales'* idea. This charming Don Agustín Viñuales, Professor of Economics, whom you know, had an interest in the person you had to examine. He asked [Pedro] Salinas for a recommendation and Salinas said: "Let Lorca give it. He's got more *PULL* with Guillén than I do." Then Viñuales asked me to do it, and *he himself* wrote the telegram. I'm weak and I let him do it. And besides, I was very flattered by Salinas' remark. Forgive me. I know that this shouldn't be done, but take into consideration that it wasn't my fault and it was an old professor of mine who was asking me to do it. I want you to be aware of my attitude so you'll be able to excuse this *transgression*. I've been doing a lot of work. Very different things, directly inspired I believe. It seems to me now that I'm beginning to glimpse the poetic quality I yearn for.

You will have noticed that everybody continues to link our names. Guillén and Lorca. This truly makes me rejoice. In spite of the envious darts they inflict upon us, we continue and will continue maintaining our posts as CAPTAINS of the new Spanish poetry. Shake on it! You and I have character, personality, something inimitable that comes from within, a *unique voice* by the grace of God.

Affectionate regards to Germaine, to my precious Teresita, to the boy, and to our friends.

An embrace for you from your always loyal

Federico

I'm sending you the program for a *gallo* session that turned out to be delightful and at which a group of Granadan youths showed one more time that Granada is the indisputable literary capital of Andalusia.

Greetings to [Juan] Guerrero [Ruiz]!
Write me!
Write me!

[1][To] Jorge Guillén. University. Murcia. [October, 1928?]

PASS AGUSTIN PELAEZ NO MATTER
WHAT. FIRST FAVOR. HUGS
CHILDREN. HUGS.

FEDERICO

TO JORGE ZALAMEA

[Autumn, 1928]

Dear Jorge:

I got your letter. I thought you were angry. I rejoice with all my poor heart (this unfortunate child of mine) to find you the same as before, as at first. You're suffering but you shouldn't. Sketch out a plan of your desire and live within it, always within a norm of beauty. That's what I do, dear friend . . . but how difficult it is for me! But I do it. I'm slightly out of sorts with the world, but the living beauty that my hands touch makes up for every displeasure. And being involved in serious emotional conflicts and nearly *overcome* by love, by society, by ugly things, I keep to my norm of happiness at all costs. I don't want them to defeat me. You shouldn't let yourself be defeated. I know very well what you're going through.

You're in a sad age of doubt and bear an artistic problem on your shoulders that you don't know how to solve. Don't worry. That problem will take care of itself. One morning you'll begin to see clearly. I know. It grieves me to know you're passing through bad times. But you should learn to overcome them one way or another. Anything is preferable to being eaten up, broken, crushed by them. By sheer will power, I've *resolved* these past few days, one of the most painful periods I've experienced in my life. You just can't imagine what it is to spend entire nights on the balcony looking at a nocturnal Granada, *empty* for me and without finding the least bit of consolation in anything.

And then . . . trying constantly to see to it that your state of mind does not filter into your poetry, because it will play you a bad trick by exposing the purest in you to the eyes of those who should *never* see it. That is why, for discipline, I'm doing these precise *academic* things now and opening my soul before the symbol of the Sacrament, and my eroticism in the "Ode to Sesostris," which I've halfway finished.

I speak of these things, because you ask me; I will speak no more of that which, external to me, wounds me from afar in the surest and most sapient way.

But I defend myself! I'm more valiant than the Cid (Campeador).[1]

This "Ode to Sesostris" will please you, because it belongs to my *furious* genre. The "Ode to the [Most Holy] Sacrament" is almost finished. And it seems to me to contain great intensity. Probably the greatest poem I've done.

The part I'm working on now (it will have a total of three hundred verses) is "Devil, second enemy of the soul," and that's strong.

> Deep blinding light of crackling matter,
> oblique light of swords and star's quicksilver,
> announced the loveless body coming
> through all the corners of open Sunday.

> Beauty's form without nostalgia nor dream.
> Murmur of liberated and mad surfaces.
> Marrow of the present. Feigned security
> of floating on the water with the marble torso.

> Body of beauty which throbs and escapes.
> A moment of veins and navel's tenderness.
> Love between walls and confined kisses,
> with the sure fear of the burning goal.

> Beautiful with light, orient of the feeling hand.
> Storm and youth of bristles and mollusks,
> fire for the sensitive flesh that burns,
> nickel for the sob that seeks God flying.

It seems to me that this "Devil" is really a Devil. Each time this part gets more obscure, more metaphysical, until at the end there surges forth the extremely cruel beauty of the enemy, a wounding beauty, enemy of love.

Adiós. I gave you the whole boring account. A very warm embrace from

Federico

Write me.

---

[1] El Cid Campeador, Rodrigo Díaz de Vivar, national hero of Spain, whose deeds are celebrated in the twelfth-century epic *El Cantar del Mio Cid* (*The Poem of the Cid*).

TO JORGE ZALAMEA

[1928]

[Fragment]

I never change my manner of speaking and this letter carries unpublished verses of mine, emotions as a friend and as a man I wouldn't want to divulge. I desire and demand my privacy. If I fear *stupid fame* it's precisely because of this. A famous man knows the bitterness of having a cold breast transfixed by deaf lanterns turned on him by *others*.

I'm deeply involved in the "Ode to the Holy Sacrament of the Altar." We'll see how it turns out. It's extremely difficult. But my faith will do it.

> Beneath the wings of the dragon there's a child,
> and in the creaking moon little horses of blood.
> The unicorn seeks what the rose forgets
> and the bird attempts what the waters impede.
> Only you, Sacrament of light in equilibrium,
> soothe the anguish of chainless love.
> Only you, Sacrament, manometer that saves
> hearts flung at five hundred per hour.

This verse "The unicorn seeks what the rose forgets," I like a lot. It has the indefinable poetic enchantment of blurred conversation.

TO CARLOS MORLA LYNCH

[Early June, 1929]

Most dear Carlos (my son):

You are charming as always. Forgive me for not writing. But I've been very busy with my trip. Carlos: this Saturday night I'm leaving Granada in order to be in Madrid Sunday morning.

I will be in Madrid for two days to take care of some last minute things and leave immediately for Paris, London, and there I will embark for New York. Are you surprised? I'm also surprised. I'm going to die laughing over this decision. But it suits me and it's an important one in my life. I will stay in America six or seven months and will return to Paris for the rest of the year. New York seems horrible, but for that very reason I'm going there. I think I'll have a very good time. I'm taking the trip with my good friend Fernando de los Ríos, my old teacher and an extremely charming person who will get me over the initial rough spots, since, as you know, I am useless and foolish when it comes to practical life.

I am very well, with a new restlessness concerning the world and my future. This trip will be very useful to me. My papa gave me all the money I need and is happy with this decision of mine.

I can't express the desire, the *hunger* I have to give you a hug (because I love you so very much), and greetings to Bebé and to your Carlitos.[1]

I also have a great desire to write, an unstoppable love for poetry, for the pure verse that fills my soul, still shuddering like a little antelope, from the last brutal arrows.

But . . . forward! No matter how insignificant I may be, I believe that I *deserve* to be loved.

Tomorrow my friends are getting together to bid me farewell. It's a party organized by the fellows from the University, and entrance will be denied to people over thirty, to avenge the banquet I was given recently which they weren't able to attend because it cost 30 *pesetas*. The price of the ticket will be 5 *pesetas* and it will be an unforgettable event.

I can't refrain from sending you a proof of the extremely

spiritual picture I had taken for the passport. Its light borders on that of a murder scene and the dark corner where the delicate pickpocket stashes his bundle of bills.

Capriciously the lens reveals a slack harp looming behind my back like a jellyfish and the whole atmosphere partakes of the finite twitching of cigar ash.

Keep it or tear it up. It's a melancholy Federico I'm sending you and the Federico that writes you is, as of now, a *Strong* Federico.

I'm happy. And I expect to embrace you soon. See you Sunday!

Hugs to our good friend Alfredo.

Federico

Death to (. . .) who is a porcupine!

[1] Morla Lynch's wife and son.

[1929]

[Fragment from on board the ship to New York]

. . . One feels depressed and full of longings. I hunger for my land and for the days in your familiar little salon. I miss chatting with you and singing you old Spanish songs.

I don't know why I left; I ask myself that question a hundred times a day. I look at myself in the mirror of the confining cabin and I don't recognize myself. I seem to be another Federico.

TO PHILLIP CUMMINGS

[July 6 or 7, 1929]

My dear friend:

I was overjoyed to receive your letter. I've found a place in New York. I want to see you soon and think of you constantly but on the advice of Professor [Federico de] Onís, I've registered at Columbia University and for this reason I can't be with you until six weeks from now. Then, if you still wish me to, I'll be delighted to come.

If you won't be at home at that time I invite you to come to see me in New York. What do you say to that? Write me in all confidence if this is possible.

I'm bewildered by your great generosity in sending me the money for the ticket and, of course, if my trip isn't arranged within the next six weeks I'll return it to you with eternal gratitude and noble friendship which is the most a Spaniard can offer.

Write me immediately and tell me what you think of the postponement of my trip. Since I'm registered I must take this course in English. Later on I could spend a few days with you and they will be delightful for me.

I hope you'll answer me and won't forget this poet from the South now lost in this Babylonic, cruel and violent city, filled on the other hand, with a great modern beauty.

I live at Columbia and my address is:

> Mister Federico G. Lorca
> Furnald Hall
> Columbia University
> New York City

I hope you will answer me right away. *Adiós,* dear friend. An embrace from Federico.

My respects to your parents.

TO ANGEL DEL RIO[1]

[Eden Mills, August, 1929]

Dear Angel:

I'm writing you from Eden Mills. Having a good time. The landscape is marvelous, but infinitely melancholy.

A good experience for me. I'll tell you all about it. Now I only want to know how to find you so as to be with you in a few days' time.

It never stops raining. This family is very nice, full of gentle charm, but the woods and lakes immerse me in a hardly bearable state of poetic desperation. I write all day and at night I feel drained.

Angel: tell me by return mail how to meet you. When I think that I can *drink* in the house where you live it makes me very happy.

Now night is falling. The oil lamps have been lit and my whole childhood comes back to me, wrapped in a glory of poppies and grainfields. Among the ferns I've found a distaff covered with spiders and in the lake not one frog sings.

Urgently need cognac for my poor heart. Write me and I'll go to meet you.

Affectionate regards to Amelia. Kisses on the feet for the child and a hug for you from your friend

Federico

(Pursued in Eden Mills by the liqueur of romanticism).

Show me the route of the trip. If it's easier for you send me a long telegram explaining it to me.

My address for the telegraph is as follows—[Phillip] Cummings will type it out.

I'd prefer it if you would send a telegram.

In any case, I'll have to pass through New York. It's likely I'll leave on Thursday. This is a haven for me, but I'm choked in this mist and this tranquillity brings my memories back in such a way that they burn me.

Addio, mio caro!

[1] Angel del Río: professor of Spanish at Columbia University, and author of *Federico García Lorca: Vida y obra,* Zaragoza, 1952.

TO MELCHOR FERNANDEZ ALMAGRO

N[ew] Y[ork], 30 Sept[ember, 1929]

Dear Melchor:

This letter has no other object than to send you an affectionate embrace with the most intense remembrance.

Although you have already *repudiated* me from afar, I feel that my friendship is true and perennial. *I've overcome my shock, I work and enjoy myself.*

I've written a book of poetry and almost another. *Fury of the Muses:* remember when you called me that, in an inn on Calle de Carmen, where [Francisco] Campos [Aravaca] lived?

I have many American friends, women and men, and am, therefore, making quick progress in English. I'm not going to do descriptions of New York for you. It's immense, but it is made for man, the human proportion adjusts to things that from far away seem gigantic and disordered.

I find I'm happy, with that happiness of recent spring and I attend those prodigious football games with the candor of a regular fan. I think this trip was the right thing to do.

I see a lot of Dámaso [Alonso] and his wife [Eulalia Galvarriato] here; he's giving a course *on us* [the "Generation of '27"] at the University. The warmest greetings to your mother and your sisters, to all the friends who *ask about me,* to [Francisco] Ayala, to [Angel] Vegue [Goldoni], to [Pedro] Salinas. I'll write Salinas tomorrow.

Adiós, Melchorito. Write me at length, and I'll respond right away. Don't forget me and here's a strong hug from yours always

Federico

Address: John Jay Hall, Columbia University, New York City.

TO CARLOS MORLA LYNCH

[New York, November, 1929]

My dear Carlos:

This letter is no more than a heartfelt embrace and an "I don't forget you." Surely you've read the second edition of my *Songs* with the dedication to your unforgettable daughter.[1] These printed lines are bonds that unite me to you forever.

I'm living at Columbia University, in the heart of New York, in a splendid place near the Hudson River. I have five classes and spend the days greatly amused as if in a dream. I spent the summer in Canada with some friends and I'm now in New York, which is a city of unexpected happiness. I've written a lot. I have almost two books of poems and a theatrical piece. I'm relaxed and happy. That Federico of old, whom you didn't know but whom I hope you'll meet, has been reborn. Write me.

Regards to B . . . with love; to dear Carlitos [Morla Vicuña] and to Alfredo, whom I admire and remember always.[2] *Adiós,* Carlos. Here goes a hug with all my heart.

Federico

(My address: John Jay Hall, Columbia University, New York.)

[1] Lynch's daughter died at an early age.
[2] Lynch's son, and the Secretary of the Chilean Embassy, respectively.

TO HIS FAMILY

[New York, January, 1930]

Dear Parents, sisters and brother:

The Christmas holidays passed with sparkle and glitter and the weather's been excellent. I've received your letters and the letters from Manolo [Fernández Montesinos] and Conchita [García Lorca] from Cordoba and Barcelona for which I'm very grateful. They ought to hold their wedding now since they haven't held it, a thing I feel sorry about, and they should have done so already since with a family as large as ours it will never be possible to celebrate anything at all in this life. You see how much better Eloísa [Palacios García] is, according to what Conchita told me. Naturally I'm happy about her recovery and I'll be eternally thankful when she recuperates completely. I hope that you spent the Holiday Season happily, as you well deserve.

I had dinner at the Onís' house on Christmas Eve. José Antonio Rubio [Sacristán] and the del Río couple (Amelia and Angel) with the great Italian critic, Prosolini [Giuseppe Prezzolini] and his son Alexander were there. The meal was very pleasant with lots of wine and good cheer, but I had to leave them at ten to go to [Herschel] Brickell's house where they had a Christmas tree and close friends of the family gathered. Naturally I had an even better time at their place. Because it's a completely different society and I feel like a foreigner there. They gave me an infinite number of presents and there I took part in a very English ceremony yet full of enchantment and family warmth. They'd set up a small altar and on a mosaic of Talavera they'd mounted as many candles as partakers. One by one we lit them and upon lighting each candle one had to make a good wish for another person. I, naturally, *wished* for your health and happiness, since although you're five people for me it's as if you're one.

Anyway, the Americans take this almost superstitious thing seriously because they're like children. Later we went to a midnight mass at the church of St. Paul where a chorus of children sang a magnificent mass and officiated with stunning solemnity.

Here I was able to see how alive Catholicism is in this country, because it has to vie with the Protestants and Jews who have their churches across the street. There were hundreds and hundreds of people at communion. It can be said that the whole cathedral received communion. And it was a typical New York crowd. Blacks, Chinese, Americans, etc.

The best Christmas Eve I've seen, of course, was at the Tomasas nunnery, or that unforgettable Christmas Eve at Asquerosa when they put a flat red hat on St. Joseph and a bullfight *mantilla* on the Virgin. But the street noise is the same. They set up loudspeakers and Christmas trees covered with lights in all the squares and the crowds go back and forth among the drunken sailors.

On the following day the *Times* said that eighty cases of severe alcohol poisoning were reported, many of whom died, naturally. Because, it's clear, New York is today, on account of Prohibition, the place where people drink more than anywhere else in the world. There are an infinite number of industries dedicated to alcohol and to poisoning the people because they make wines with wood and chemical substances that leave people blind or corrode their kidneys. Oh horror! It's perfectly clear that this is an imposition of the odious Methodist Church, much worse than the Spanish Jesuits in the present historical phase. Because the entire State of New York has never been dry but *wet* and because of this alone they succeed in making out of a clean and common drink a new artificial paradise, which everyone covets and the number of drunks is much greater than before. Of course, I don't drink anything unless I make sure that it's all right and besides the houses to which I go where drinks are served are distinguished houses and they offer excellent quality. It's a sure thing now that I'm going to Cuba in the month of March. Onís has arranged the trip for me. There I'll give eight or ten lectures. I'd like you to send me the lecture on Góngora.[1] If you can't find it, I think that [Enrique Gómez] Arboleya has it. Of course I won't give it as it is, but it will serve as a basis for one that I'm writing. And send me also, if you have it, the lecture on *Cante Jondo*. Not to deliver it as is, but to gather the ideas from it. Since this is a very important subject I'm going to present it as a polemic, not only in Cuba, but later in Madrid, this matter of *Cante Jondo* and Andalusian poetry.

I'm working steadily. I'm writing a book of poems of interpretations of New York which makes an enormous impression on my friends because of its forcefulness. I believe that everything of mine pales alongside these things which in a certain way are *symphonic* like the noise and complexity of New York.

Greetings to everybody. Especially to Aunt Isabel [García Rodríguez]. To the whole family, to Eduarda [Miranda Lorca], to the girls, and for you hugs and kisses from your son,

Federico

You agreed to tell me about the wedding, but you haven't told me anything, since what you did tell me I already knew or imagined.

Hugs! Kisses!

---

[1] Included in *Deep Song and Other Prose,* translated and edited by Christopher Maurer, New York, 1980.

TO ENCARNACION LOPEZ JULVEZ, LA ARGENTINITA

[Granada, Summer, 1931]

[Drawing: Spanish lady]

Dear Godmother:[1]

Since I couldn't say good-bye to you on account of my illness, and since you called me on the phone and then you weren't home, I write to greet you with great affection and admiration, and to tell you that I live at Acera del Casino 31, Granada, ready to serve you in whatever way I can.

I'm totally involved in my work now and very happy with this landscape and with this enchanting family of mine.

I recall you constantly, since my sisters, who are *fervent* admirers of yours, put on your records, which are, in parenthesis, stupendous, at every opportunity.

What about Ignacio [Sánchez Mejías]? Give him a hug for me. I hope that you will remember me in your prayers and won't forget me.

For you, dear Godmother of my soul, the most affectionate greeting from your collaborator and companion

Federico García Lorca

—Granada—

What's happening with the records?[2] I haven't gotten stamps. Do you want to ask Gelabert? Cora is something horrible!

---

[1] Refers to her role as Godmother of Federico de Onís' son; Lorca was his Godfather.

[2] A collection of popular old folk songs, with Lorca at the piano and La Argentinita singing.

TO CARLOS MORLA LYNCH

[Granada, Summer, 1931]

My dear ones:

I wrote you and you didn't respond. What's happening? I read about the revolution in Chile[1] and worry a lot about you.

What sort of Government is it? Do you have any idea of your new situation? Write and tell me everything. I want to know.

I'm working a lot. At the end of September I'll do a reading in your house (which is mine, as you've always told me) of my new play with guests and photos.

I received your postcards from Sigüenza with the whole gang. I hope that Carlos will have finally given my regards to ineffable A's missus . . .

Right now my house is full of lullabies for the little girl and my mother, my sisters, my father, and the trees and the dogs are all asleep, all except the little girl who never sleeps.

I love you so much, that I want a portrait of Carlos to put with that of Bebé's on the sides of my desk, the way it's done in church, the Sacred Heart of Jesus (on the left) and the Sacred Heart of Mary (on the right).

Oh, how hot it is! But what a good heat, golden, full of birds and hard green leaves.

Write me telling me everything.

A thousand kisses and hugs from your

Federico

Regards to all our friends.

---

[1] Carlos Ibañez del Campo, military dictator of Chile, was forced into exile in 1931, and the previous president, Alessandri Palma, a liberal, was re-elected in 1932.

TO CARLOS MORLA LYNCH

[Granada, Summer, 1931]

Dear Carlos:

I received your letter. I don't forget you for a moment. I always look at the delightful portrait of Bebé that I have on my desk; on her bosom lies a white bear's paw, a cauliflower, or a piece of snow, depending on whether one feels epic, comic or lyric.

At times I undergo intense attacks of affection that I cure by drinking Granadan wine in the admirable Moorish gardens of the Chirimías and remembering you amidst the fragrance of the myrtles.

I work. I'm already on the third act of *When Five Years Pass,* whose idea Bebé liked so much.

I hope we'll read it soon and if you like it, nothing will make me happier.

I congratulate (congratulate?) you with all my heart for the events in Chile . . . but my heart breaks thinking that you might have to go. I understand the rightness of your being minister and that Bebé can use her by now melancholy court dress for other marble floors, but egotistically I'd like to have you by my side so I can come late to dinner and set up Bebé's bed in the living room. *Ay!*

I hope you'll answer me immediately.

Kisses, hugs and tears from

Federico

TO CARLOS MORLA LYNCH

[Granada, latter half of August, 1931]

Dear Carlos:

What grief![1] All day long I thought of you. In my house, the same. When I told my mother the enchanting words of Gitanillo about the Virgin, she cried, and a woman who was there sewing, very Andalusian, said: "God bless him, you can be sure he is now in the Virgin's arms!"[2]

It has been a grievous pain, and I can imagine how you must have suffered, and I'm with you because I understand you and because I too am accustomed to suffer because of things which people don't understand or suspect.

Between one person and another there are spider threads that little by little turn into wires and even bars of steel. When death separates us there remains a bloody wound in the place of each thread.

You must know I don't forget you for a moment and I wish I could embrace you with the tenderness and lyric foolishness I feel for you. Tenderness because it comes from the blood and foolishness (oh, sweet silliness and divine blather of infants!) because it comes from the soul, which is the most foolish of our possessions.

But I want you to be strong, because it hurts me that you should add sufferings to the many you've had, although I know this is impossible in a heart so great and elevated as yours. God too has to be good to you, and the same with the Virgin, the Holy Virgin, full of swords like a bull, who shelters the *toreros* and who takes to herself those who are handsome and good as was Gitanillo.

Carlos, I embrace you with all my affection. Regards to Bebé and to Carlitos. And tell Rafael [Martínez Nadal] that his treatment of me is vile. I haven't done anything to him and he hasn't answered my last four letters. I'm really hurt. He's either bad or irresponsible. I'd gladly punch him. I'm fit to bust.

Adiós, Carlitos. A thousand embraces for you and write me a lot.

Federico

[1] The death of the bullfighter Gitanillo (Little Gypsy) de Triana.
[2] Gitanillo de Triana told Lynch, "I'll tell the Virgin how good you've been to me." (C. M. Lynch's *En España con Federico García Lorca,* Madrid, 1957, p. 71.)

TO CARLOS MORLA LYNCH

[Granada, latter half of August, 1931]

Dear Carlos:

Your last letter, so beautiful, made me see how badly you've taken it and what a silent Calvary you have suffered. But, even more, it has made me see how good you are. Very few people are capable of doing what you've done; but the man who possesses these sentiments possesses, without doubt, the true treasure of the world. A treasure which is suffering, but suffering which is liberation and is, in the final analysis, heaven!

All religions have and have always had the same map. The splendor of life is for the one bearing a bucket of tears and not for the one carrying a fistful of diamonds. I wrote you another letter that crossed yours in the mail. The object of this one is to send you my affection. Besides, I desire to see you more than ever and I hope it'll be soon. *Adiós,* Carlos. Try to calm your feelings and accept a tender embrace from yours always

Federico

TO CARLOS MORLA LYNCH

[Granada, end of August, 1931]

Again I send you regards because I know that you're sad and you know how much I love you and how close you always are to me. I want to see you and I always find this paper cold, in spite of the fact that my hands are resting sweetly on its surface.

About the 15th or the 20th of September I'll be in Madrid so that there is less than a month before we'll meet again in your house, something which I look forward to eagerly; it seems the best thing that can happen to me.

I adore Bebé. So much do I adore her that she'll never know of the thousands of photographs of her deeds and her divine postures which I conserve in my imagination. Clothes, gestures, words, and even if sometimes there's a run in her stocking, I have tenderly tucked it away.

I also have a great affection for the bathroom in your house, because no one feels that way about these kinds of rooms and no one wants to talk about them; nevertheless, where I've felt myself most fully at home has been while stretched out in the bathtub while you were combing your hair and Carlitos pomaded his hair, and Bebé shouted: "Come and eat!"

It's a splendid day. A fresh murmur of cornfields and water reaches my room. I always remember you. I accompany you with my affection.

Federico

TO REGINO SAINZ DE LA MAZA

[Granada? 1931]

[Drawing: Harlequin with a sign escaping from his mouth: "Greetings to Josefina and Regino."]

Dear Regino:

I didn't want to answer you before because I didn't know what to tell you. Now I do. I've finished my work *When Five Years Pass*. I am satisfied in *a certain way* and the drama [*Yerma*] for Xirgu is half done. An effort, Regino! Besides, I've written a book of poems, *Poems for the Dead*,[1] the most intense that have left my hand. I've been like a fountain. Writing day and night. At times I've had a fever like the old romantics, but without losing that immense conscious happiness of creating.

Now I ask you: When do you want me to go after the eighth? I would like to give a lecture in Torrelavega and one in Santander and if you can in some other place. I'm telling you this because you're my *manager* now and always do the things that I can't, or that I have a certain fear of doing.

I will spend a few days with you and read you some new things. Answer me and, if you can, make the overtures.

Greetings to Josefina [de la Serna], to Miss Concha [Espina], to the enchanting Luis París [Luis de la Serna], whom I've *spotted* in a play, and to everyone.

Answer soon. So I know whether to prepare or not to prepare. A thousand hugs and regards from your

Federico (*pico chico*)[2]

Cossío told me with great insistence that I should notify him of my arrival.

---

[1] *Poemas para los muertos* was an early title for *Poeta en Nueva York*.
[2] A "little beak" asking for favors.

TO MIGUEL HERNANDEZ

[1933]

My dear poet:

I've not forgotten you. But I'm too busy living and the pen for writing letters gets away from me.

I remember you often because I know that you suffer with those swinish people surrounding you and it is painful for me to see your vital and luminous strength enclosed in a corral and butting against the barriers.

But that's the way you learn. That's the way you learn to master yourself in this terrible apprenticeship life is giving you. Your book is bound in silence, like all first books, like my first book, that had so much charm and so much strength. Write, read, study. FIGHT! Don't be vain about your work. Your book is strong, it contains many interesting things and reveals to good eyes *a manly passion,* but it has no more *cojones,* as you say, than those of nearly all the consecrated poets. Calm yourself. Today Spain is producing the most beautiful poetry in Europe. But on the other hand the public is unjust. *Perito en lunas (Expert in Mirrors)* doesn't deserve this stupid silence, no. It deserves the attention and the encouragement and the love of all. Which you have and will have because you have the blood of a poet, and even when you protest in your letter, you possess amidst brutal things (which I like) the tenderness of your luminous and tormented heart.

I should like you to be able to overcome the obsession, that obsession of misunderstood poet, for another more generous political and poetic obsession. Write me. I want to speak to several friends to see if they will take an interest in *Perito en lunas.*

Books of poetry, dear Miguel, make headway very slowly.

I understand you perfectly and send you my fraternal embrace, full of affection and camaraderie.

Federico

(Write me.)
To Alcalá, 102.

TO EZIO LEVI

[September, 1934]

My dear friend:

I've received your letters and today I've received one from [Luigi] Pirandello and Marconi [?] inviting me to the Theater Congress in Rome. I'm very pleased and grateful for the invitation because I consider it a great honor. A few days ago I wrote to Madrid asking them when they were starting rehearsals for my work *Yerma,* which they're thinking of premiering next November, but they haven't answered me. Today I'm writing another [. . .] of a very urgent nature. That is why I have not answered. If within two days I haven't received a reply or if I've received a negative one, I'll write you definitively and I'll send my definitive reply to the Academy. I would very much like to go.

Do you think that the Congress would be interested in the topic of "La Barraca"?[1] Tell me frankly, so I can think up another topic. I still have time to put off my reply a couple of days. If it's too late, tell me that as well.

I don't have photos of "La Barraca," because I keep them in Madrid; but I'll ask for whatever is available. The Congress[2] asks me to bring along my wife, but since I don't have one, can I bring along the secretary of "La Barraca," who is also my personal secretary [Rafael Rodríguez Rapún]? Tell me what you think about all these questions.

You know that I'm intense and not a very social person and I'm also a little afraid of all official things. I have an infantile character and it will be good to be alongside so many brilliant people. How should I *focus* the topic of "La Barraca" for the Congress?

A thousand pardons from your friend who loves you and sends you an affectionate embrace. *Adiós.*

Federico García Lorca

[1] La Barraca: traveling theater troop, in which Lorca was involved in the early 1930s, which brought classical Spanish theater to the provinces.
[2] The Writers' Congress in Rome of which Ezio Levi was Secretary.

TO ANGEL FERRANT

[1935]

My dear friend and *collaborator*:

I'd like, if you can and it's possible, if you could do me the favor of modeling the little puppet heads.[1] Time is running out and I wouldn't like to be on the bad side of those people from my old Residencia.

The head of Cristóbal is energetic, brutal, like the club.

Currito el der Puerto is young with a very melancholy character.

Cocoliche is the beautiful child, *the singer*.

The Mosquito is Shakespeare's Puck, half sprite, half child, *half insect*.

Fígaro is a Fígaro.

I ask you not to forget me and to tell me where we could sketch them out.

I hope to hear from you quickly.

Meanwhile, here's a cordial embrace of affection and admiration from your companion

Federico

---

[1] For a puppet play *Retablillo de Don Cristóbal* produced in the Teatro de la Zarzuela, Madrid, 1937.

TO ADOLFO SALAZAR

[Madrid, first part of June, 1936]
(Urgent)

Little Lord Musician
Adolfito Salazar,
              from your friend
Federico

Dear Adolfo:

I'm going to Granada for two days to take leave of my family. Since I'm going by car, it was arranged in a hurry and I didn't say anything to you.

I would like it if you could, and without Bagaría[1] noticing it, remove the question and answer that's on a loose handwritten page, page 7 (*bis*), because it's an aside and it's a question about Fascism and Communism that seems to me indiscreet at this juncture, and besides it was already answered previously. So then, you remove it and it'll be as if nothing happened. It's not befitting that anyone find out about this, since it would be troublesome for me.[2]

Hugs.

                                                            Federico

---

[1] Luis Bagaría (1882–1940): caricaturist and interviewer for the Madrid daily, *El Sol.*

[2] This letter was hand delivered by an intermediary; it bears no stamp or address. Since the occasion for Lorca's leavetaking (his trip to Mexico) didn't take place, this trip to Granada was called off. The question and answer referred to were omitted from the printed interview in *El Sol.* Thus, Lorca maintained his posture of radical independence despite pressure from friends to adopt a specific political affiliation.

Before returning to Granada in July, he told Martínez Nadal: "Rafael, those fields are going to be filled with the dead." (Rafael Martínez Nadal, *El Público, Amor y muerto en la obra de Federico García Lorca,* Mexico, 1974, p. 12.)

Index

Names of the recipients of the letters, along with page numbers for each letter to a given individual, are printed in boldface.

Aben-Humeya, 29
Abentofail, 33, 34
"Academy of the Rose and the Jar of Ink," 133
Alberti, Rafael, vii, viii
Alcalde, 5
Aleixandre, Vincente, vii, viii
Alhambra, 23, 36, 54
"*Al oido de una muchacha*" ("To a Girl's Ear"), 54
Alonso, Dámaso, 151
Alonso, Eulalia Galvarriato (wife), 151
Altolaguirre, Manolo, vii
Alvarez de Cienfuegos, Antonio, 34, 76
"*Amanecer y repique*" ("Dawn and Bell-toll"), 42
Amarilis (shepherdess), 41
America, xi, 27, 124, 146
Amigo Aguado, Joaquín, 131
Andalusia, v, vii, 32, 39, 44, 56, 61, 64, 72–73, 78, 80, 116, 128, 131, 139, 154, 159
Angeles Ortiz, Manuel, 16, 17, 29, 30, 34, 76, 131, 134, 136
"Another Small Sketch" ("*Otra estampita*"), 42
"Anti-Artistic Manifesto," x
Aragón, 69
Aragon, Louis, viii
"*Arco de lunas*" ("Moon Haloes"), 42
Argentina, xii
Así que pasen cinco años (*When Five Years Pass*), xi, 47n, 158, 162
Asquerosa, 14, 22, 154
Atheneum of Barcelona, 58
Atheneum of Murcia, 58
Aubry, Jean, 25, 28
Ayala, Francisco, 123, 151

Baeza, 1n
Bagaría, Luis, 166
"Ballad of Antoñito el Camborio," 94, 98
"Ballad of the Martyrdom of the Gypsy Saint Olalla of Mérida," 93
"Ballad of the Spanish Civil Guard" ("*Romance de la Guardia Civil Española*"), 93
Barcelona, vi, ix, 58, 69, 110, 124, 125, 135
Bárcena, Catalina, 48, 57
Barradas, Rafael, 31
Barrios, Angel, 15n, 24n, 31
"Beaten Gypsy," 72
Bello, José, 54, **61**
Bergamín, José, vii, viii, x, 62, **107**
Berrueta, Martín Domínguez, 52
Billy Club Puppets of Granada, 19, 27, 29, 35, 39, 42
Blasco Ibáñez, Vincente, 57
Bodas de sangre (*Blood Wedding*), xii
Book of Poems (*Libro de poemas*), 14, 15n, 20n, 24n, 28
"Brawl" ("*Reyerta de mozos*"), 85
Brickell, Herschel, 153
Buenos Aires, xii
Burgos, 52

Cadaqués, viii, 59, 64, 65, 111, 113
Campos Aravaca, Francisco, 34, 151
Canada, 152
"*Canción cantada*" ("Song Sung"), 54
"*Canción del Arbolé*" ("Song of the Tree"), 54
"*Cancionella del niño que no nacio*" ("Little Song of the Unborn Child"), 42

Canciones (Songs), 91n, 94, 98, 104, 152
Cante Jondo, 25, 30, 154
Cassou, Jean, 78
Castile, 33, 61, 69
Catalan, x, 115
Catalonia, 65, 69, 112, 115, 128, 131, 132, 134, 136
Cernuda, Luis, vii
Chacón y Calvo, José Maria, 68
Chile, vi, 157, 158
Chopin, 1, 66
Cierva y Peñafiel, Juan de la, 2, 4
Ciria y Escalante, José de, 22, 26, 34, **37, 41,** 50, 51n, 52–53
Civil War, Spanish, viii, xii
Cocoliche (puppet character), 165
Columbia University (New York), xi, 149, 152
Communism, 166
Cossio, José Maria, 98, 162
Cristóbal, Don Juan, 19, 20n, 27, 29, 34, 71, 165
Cristobicas (puppet show), 32
Cuba, xi, 154
Cummings, Phillip, 149, 150
Curie, Marie, viii
Currito er der Puerto, 19, 165

Dalí, Ana María (sister), ix, **59, 64, 66, 77, 110, 113, 122**
Dalí, Salvador, viii, ix, x, xi, 59–60, 65, 69, 76, 77, 101, 104, 107, 110, 111, 112, 113, 114, 118, 123, 124, 125, 128, 131, 133, 134, 135, 136
Dalmau Galleries (Barcelona), ix
Darro (river), 12, 23
"Dawn and Bell-toll" (*"Amanecer y repique"*), 42
"Daydreams of the River," 35
Defensor de Granada (magazine), 88, 101, 107
"Diálogo de la bicicleta de Filadelphia" ("The Dialogue of the Philadelphia Bicycle"), 62
"Diálogo de la danza" ("Dialogue of the Dance"), 62
"Didactic Ode to Salvador Dali," 73
"Diego Corrientes," 86
Diego, Gerardo, vii, viii, **27, 37, 41,** 42, 78, 88
Díez-Canedo, Enrique, 17, 40, 57
Domínquez Berrueta, Martín, 7
Don Juan Tenorio (Zorrilla), 57

"Don Lindo of Almeria" (José Bergamín), 108
Don Quixote, 64–65
d'Ors, Eugenio ("Xenius"), 45, 64–65, 65n, 94, 95
Drawings (Lorca), ix, 119–120, 121, 125, 128, 134, 136

"Earth/Sky" (*"Tierra/Cielo"*), 42
Eden Mills (Vermont), 150
Elegias verdaderas (True Elegies), 9
El gallo del Defensor (magazine), x, 101–102, 103, 107, 125, 126, 128, 129, 131, 132, 134, 139, 142
"El loco y la loca" ("The Madman and the Madwoman"), 62
El Lombardo (gypsy), 18
El Público, xi
El sacrificio de Ifigenia, 64
"El sátiro blanco" ("The White Satyr"), 42
El Sol (newspaper), 20n, 166n
"El teniente coronal de la Guardia Civil" ("The Lieutenant Colonel of the Civil Guard"), 62
El último (café), 33, 34n
"Erotic Hallelujahs in Three Scenes," 55, 56n
Espina, Concha, 162
"Es verdad" ("It is True"), 54
Europe, 27, 54, 130

"Fable and Round of the Three Friends," xii
Fajardo, Enrique ("Fabian Vidal"), 100
Falangists, xii
Falla, María del Carmen (sister), 26, 29, 43, 112
Fascism, 166
Falla, Manuel de, ix, 25, 26–27, 28, **29,** 31, 32, 35, 41–42, **43,** 46, 53, 101, 107, **112,** 118
Fernández Almagro, Melchor, vii, x, **14, 15, 21, 23, 30, 32, 33, 34, 37, 39, 44, 46,** 48, **50,** 51n, **52, 54, 55,** 57, **62, 63, 69, 71, 76, 88, 92,** 93, 95, **97, 100, 111, 123, 151**
Fernández-Montesinos García, Manuel (nephew), 4n, 8n, 153
Ferrant, Angel, 165
Fígaro (puppet character), 165
Filín, 61

Folk ballads, Spanish, ix, 98
Folk dances, Spanish, 18, 26
Folk songs, Granadan, 3, 18, 25, 26, 98
Font, Manuel, 132
France, 3, 77
Frasquito er de La Fuente (gypsy), 18
Fury of the Muses, 151

Gaceta literaria (magazine), 124, 126
Gallego Burín, Antonio, 7, 48
García Lorca, Concha (sister), 153, 156
García Lorca (family), vii, 14, 17, 57, 153
García Lorca, Francisco (brother), x, 6, 8, 24, 26, 27, 30, 58, 61, 70, 77, 81, 102, 108, 113, 119, 128, 129
García Lorca, Isabela (sister), 2, 32, 50, 156
García Maroto, Gabriel, 19, 23
García Rodríguez, Enrique (uncle), 14
García Rodríguez, Federico (father), 7, 29
García Rodríguez, Isabel (aunt), 155
García Valdecasas, Alfonso, viii, 27, 63
García Vela, Fernando, 103
Gasch, Sebastián, vi, vii, ix, x, **115, 116, 117, 118, 119, 121, 124, 126, 128, 131, 134, 135, 136, 138**
"Generation of '27," vii, 27n, 151
Gerhard, Roberto, 16, 19, 28
Gitanillo de Triana, 159, 159n
Glinka, Mikhail, 42
Gómez Arboleya, Enrique, 102, 154
Gómez de la Serna, Ramón, 22
Gómez Orbaneja, 85
Góngora, Luis de, vii, 72, 75, 75n, 104, 154
Gonzalez de la Serna, Ismael, 11n
Granada, ix, x, xi, 5, 12, 14, 16, 19, 23, 27, 28, 32, 34, 35, 39, 40, 44, 45, 48, 50, 54, 56, 62, 64, 65, 66–67, 74, 75, **76, 82, 84, 89, 90, 92, 103, 112, 113, 115, 123, 124, 125, 126, 131, 133, 134, 135, 136, 139, 142, 146, 156, 158, 166**
Granada (magazine), 74, 76
Granadan Arabic culture, 33–34
Granadan *cancionero*, 89
Granada, Plain of, 9, 14
Granada, University of, ix, 16, 32, 126
Granja (café), 123
Guadalquivir (river), 35
Guerrero, María, 123

Guerrero Ruiz, Juan, 73, 96, 101, 103, 106, 109, 142
Guillén, Claudio (son), 80, 83, 109, 129
Guillén, Germaine (wife), 78, 80, 85, 95, 96, 103, 106, 109, 129, 141
Guillén, Jorge, vi, vii, x, 62, 70, **72,** 76, **78, 80, 82,** 84, 88, **93, 94,** 97, **101, 104, 109, 129, 141**
Guillén, Teresa (daughter), 62, 70, 72, 80, 83, 95, 101, 104, 109, 129, 141
Gypsies, x, 18, 26
Gypsy Ballads (Romancero gitano), x, xi, 39, 72–73, 80, 85, 92, 93, 111, 124, 136

Halffter, Ernesto, 42, 65
Harlem, xi
Hernández, Miguel, xii, **163**
Homage to Debussy (Falla), 43
Horta, Salvador de, 113
Huerta de San Vicente, 82, 113, 121, 139

Ibañez del Campo, Carlos, 157n
Icaza, Francisco A. de, 58
Impresiones y paisajes (Impressions and Landscapes), 96n, 97
Indice (Magazine), 14, 16, 19, 21, 23, 26, 27n
Islam, 34
"It is True" (*"Es verdad"*), 54

Jacob, Max, viii
Jammes, Francis, 9
Jarnés, Benjamín, 102
Jiménez, Juan Ramón, 26, 27n, 50, 51n, 85, 95
Jiménez, Zenobia (wife), 50
John Jay Hall, xi, 151

La Alpujarra, 29, 31, 129
"La Argentinita" (Encarnación López Julvez), ix, **156**
La Barraca, xi, 164
"La doncella, el marinero y el estudiante" ("The Maiden, the Sailor and the Student"), 62
La Epoca (journal), 100
"Lament of the Voiceless Girl," 37
L'Amic de les Arts, 113, 127, 128, 134, 136
Lanjarón, 113, 116, 119, 121
Lanz, Hermenegildo, 112

Latin America, xi, xii
La Voz (journal), 100, 123
La Zapatera prodigiosa (The Shoe-maker's Prodigious Wife), xi, 39, 57, 123
Levi, Ezio, 164
Libro de poemas (Book of Poems), 14, 15n, 20n, 24n, 28
Litoral (magazine), 94, 95, 98
"Little Song of the Unborn Child" *("Cancionella del niño que no nacio")*, 42
Llanos Medina, Emilia, 11, 12
Lola y Lola (Gómez Arboleya), 102
London, 28, 146
Lopez Julvez, Encarnation ("La Argentinita"), ix, 156
Lumbreras, Francisco Martínez, 100
Luna García, Antonio, viii, 63, 108
Lydia (local character), 59, 64–65, 113

Machado, Antonio, 58
Madrid, ix, xii, 7, 12, 21, 22, 25, 26, 28, 30, 31, 33, 34, 50, 62, 64, 65, 70, 75, 97, 108, 123, 124, 125, 133, 134, 146, 161, 164
Magazine *(Indice)*, 14, 16, 19, 21, 23, 26, 27n
Málaga, 39, 56, 64, 65, 98, 113
Marconi, 164
Marianita Pineda (legendary character), 44–45, 48, 98
Mariana Pineda (play), 46, 57, 71, 81, 89–90, 92, 97, 100, 101, 112
Marquina, Eduardo, 57, 58, 81, 89–90, 92, 114, 122
Martínez Sierra, Gregorio, 48, 57, 71
Mediterranean, vii, 65, 66, 69, 80, 116, 118, 128, 136
Menéndez Pidal, Ramón, viii
Mercure (magazine), 78
Mexico, 166n
Milan, 28
Miño (river), 35
Miranda Lorca, Eduarda, 155
Montanyá, Luis, x, 126, 131, 132, 137
"Moon Haloes" *("Arco de lunas")*, 42
Mora Guarnido, José, 14, 29, 32
Morell Márquez, Eloísa, 49
Morla Lynch, Bebé (wife), 146, 157, 158, 159, 161
Morla Lynch, Carlos, vi, vii, xi, 146, 148, 152, 157, 158, 159, 160, 161

Morla Vicuña, Carlos (son), 146, 152, 157, 159, 161
Murcia, 73, 74, 129

"Nadadora sumergida" ("Swimmer Submerged"), 135
Navarro Pardo, José, x, 8, 34
Neruda, Pablo, vi, vii
New York, xi, 146, 149, 150, 151, 152, 154, 155

"Ode," 78, 89
"Ode to Juan Belmonte," 89
"Ode to Sesotris," 134, 143–144
"Ode to the Most Holy Sacrament of the Altar," 123, 134, 144, 145
Onís, Federico de, 149, 153, 154, 156n
"On the Death of José de Ciria y Escalante," 53
Ortega y Gasset, José, viii, 8, 103
"Otra estampita" ("Another Small Sketch"), 42
Oxford, viii, 61, 81

Palacios García, Eloisa, 153
Palma, Alessandri, 157n
Paradise Closed To Many, Gardens Open To Few (Soto de Rojas), 128
Paris, 77, 146
"Pathos of the Spanish Lullaby" (lecture), 123
Peinado Chica, 17
Pelaez, Augustín, 141
Pepe-Hillo, 29, 98
Pérez de Ayala, 58
Pérez Ferrero, Miguel, 123
Perito en lunas (Expert in Mirrors) (Miguel Hernández), 163
Picasso, Pablo, x, 126, 128, 131–132, 136
Pirandello, Luigi, 164
Pitin, Luis, 102
Pizarro Zambrano, Miguel, 30
Play of the Three Wise Men (anon.), 32
Pléiade, vii
Poema del otoño infantil (Poem of the Infant Autumn), 9
Poemas para los muertos (Poems for the Dead), 162
Poem of the Cante Jondo, 25, 43
Poem of the Cid, 37
Poeta en Nueva York (Poet in New York), xi, xii, 162n

"Portico," 42
Prados, Emilio, 88, 89, 94–95
"Preciosa and the Wind," 72
Prezzolini, Giuseppe, 153
Prohibition, 154
Puig y Pujades, Josep, 60, 113
Puppet shows, 27, 29, 32, 71

Ravel, Maurice, 27
Regina (café), 62
Reposo Urquia, Maria del, 1
Residencia de Estudiantes, viii, 11,
    123, 165
Retablillo de Don Cristóbal, 165n
"*Reyerta de mozos*" ("Brawl"), 85
Rio, Amelia del (wife), 153
Rio, Angel del, 150, 153
Ríos, Fernando de los, xi, 57, 146
Rivas Cherif, Cipriano, 40, 71
Rodríguez de Arrufat, Genoveva, 12
Rodríguez Murciano, Francisco, 43,
    43n
Rodríguez Rapún, Rafael, 164
"*Romance de la Guardia Civil
    Española*" ("Ballad of the Spanish
    Civil Guard"), 93
Romancero gitano (Gypsy Ballads), x,
    xi, 39, 72–73, 80, 85, 92, 93, 111, 124,
    136
"Rose," 21
Rubio Sacristán, José Antonio, 153
Rusiñol, Santiago, 67

Sabater, Victor, 132
"Sacramental plays," 112
Sagarra, José María de, 69
**Sainz de la Maza, Regino, 5, 28, 31,
    162**
Salazar, Adolfo, 16, 17, 20n, **25,** 42,
    166
Salinas, Pedro, vii, 57, 70, 82, 83, 86,
    88, 93, 95, 97, 102, 141, 151
Sánchez Mejías, Ignacio, 156
"*San Miguel Arcangel,*" 85
"San Sebastián" (Dalí), 113, 115, 128
Santander, 162
Savoy (café), 55
"School," 21
Señá Rosita, 19, 29
Serna, Josefina de la (wife), 162
Serna, Luis de la, 162
Sierra, 89, 90, 136
Sierra Nevada, 18, 25, 80, 116, 130
"Solitude," 75, 104

Song Book of Salamanca (folkloric
    collection), 98
"Song of the Boy with Seven Hearts,"
    37
"Song of the Phantom Fire" (Falla),
    26
"Song of the Soldier," 4
"Song of the Tree" ("*Canción del
    Arbolé*"), 54
Songs (Canciones), 91n, 94, 98, 104, 152
"Song sung" ("*Canción cantada*"), 54
Soriano Lapresa, Francisco, 33, 34
Soto de Rojas, Pedro, 88, 128
Spain, vi, viii, xi, 1, 124
St. Francis of Assisi, 10
Stravinsky, Igor, 26, 27, 32
"*Suicido en Alejandria*" ("Suicide in
    Alexandria"), 135
"Suite of the Return," 46
Suites, 18, 25, 41, 46
Sur, 32
"Swimmer Submerged" ("*Nadadora
    sumergida*"), 135

Teatro de la Zarzuela, Madrid, 165n
"The Baby Poplars," 7
"The Child Who Waters the Basil
    and the Nosy Prince," 32
"The Death of the Dauro," 15
"The Dialogue of the Philadelphia
    Bicycle" ("*Diálogo de la bicicleta
    de Filadelphia*"), 62
"The Elegy of the Toads," 10
"The Game of the Mad Child and the
    Bird without a Nest," 46
"The Garden of the Moon's Grape-
    fruit," 37, 41
"The Lieutenant Colonel of the Civil
    Guard" ("*El teniente coronal de la
    Guardia Civil*"), 62
The Little Corner (*El rinconcillo*,
    café), 21, 33–34
"The Madman and the Madwoman"
    ("*El loco y la loca*"), 62
"The Maiden, the Sailor and the
    Student" ("*La doncella, el
    marinero y el estudiante*"), 62
"The Meditations and Allegories of
    Water," 35
The Mosquito (puppet character), 165
"The Myth of Saint Sebastian" (lec-
    ture), 85
*The Shoemaker's Prodigious Wife (La
    zapatera prodigiosa)*, xi, 39, 57, 123

"The Siren and the Soldier," 73
The Solitudes (*Las Soledades,* Góngora), 72, 75n
The Talkers (Cervantes), 32
"The White Satyr" ("*El sátiro blanco*"), 42
Tegeiro Llanos, Federico, 13n
"*Tierra/Cielo*" ("Earth/Sky"), 42
Torre, Claudio de la, 50
Torre, Guillermo de, vii, viii, 109
Torrelevega, 162
Tragicomedia de don Cristóbal y la Señá Rosita, 20n
True Elegies (*Elegías verdaderas*), 9

Unamuno, Miguel de, 9
"Unfaithful Wife," 72
Ultraístas, 41, 42n

Valéry, Paul, viii
Valle, Adriano del, 2, 9, 43
Valle-Inclán, Ramón Maria del, 92
Valparaiso, 12
Vassar College, xi

Vegue Goldoni, Angel, 151
Verlaine, 2
Vermont, xi
Verso y Prosa (magazine), 94, 95, 103, 109
Viaje a la luna, xi
Viñuales, Don Agustín, 141
Viznar, xii

When Five Years Pass (*Así que pasen cinco años*), xi, 47n, 158, 162
Writers' Congress, Rome, 164, 164n

Xirgu, Margarita (actress), 81, 89–90, 100, 101, 162

Yerma, xi, 162, 164

Zalamea, Jorge, vii, x, xi, **133, 139, 143, 145**
Zamora, Marichu, 14
Zaragoza, 69
Zorrilla, José, 57